Building Wealth

The 50 Best Dividend Stocks to Buy without a Broker

Mkemo London

Building Wealth with $50

Copyright ©2010 by Mkemo London
All rights reserved

Printed in the United States of America

ISBN: 978-1-453-76750-4

For more information log on to: www.investing50.com

No part of this book may be reproduced, copied or stored in any form without the expressed written permission from the publisher.

Liability Disclaimer: This publication is intended to educate the reader on financial topics and provide material that will be helpful in making informed financial decisions. No recommendation for or against any participation in a company's plan is either intended or implied. Neither the author nor the publisher takes any responsibility for any gains or losses sustained as a result of any information found in this publication. The accuracy of this publication is subject to the information and procedures available at the time of print. Always contact any institution before investing for up to date information.

To Niambi, my wife, friend and partner

Contents

Introduction   i

Part I
Getting Started
    The Basics of Stock Investing   1
    Indexes   3
    Real Estate Investment Trusts   5
    Retirement Investing   6

Part II
Direct Stock Purchase Plans (DSPPs)
    Transfer Agents   8
    Enrolling in the Plans   9
    Statements and Taxes   12

Part III
Investing with Just $50

    1   Aetna, Inc.   14
    2   Altria Group, Inc.   16
    3   American Electric Power Company, Inc.   18
    4   Aqua America, Inc.   20
    5   Bank of South Carolina Corporation   22
    6   Becton, Dickinson and Company   24
    7   Best Buy Company, Inc.   26
    8   Campbell Soup Company   28
    9   Caterpillar, Inc.   30
   10   Chemical Financial Corporation   32
   11   CH Energy Group, Inc.   34
   12   Chevron Corporation   36
   13   Clorox Company (The)   38
   14   Coca Cola Company (The)   40
   15   Colonial Properties Trust   42
   16   ConocoPhillips   44
   17   Costco Wholesale Corporation   46
   18   Dr. Pepper Snapple Group, Inc.   48
   19   Entertainment Properties Trust   50
   20   Exxon Mobil Corporation   52
   21   Frontier Communications Corporation   54

Contents

22 Glimcher Realty Trust   56
23 Hershey Company (The)   58
24 Home Depot, Inc. (The)   60
25 IBM Corporation   62
26 Intel Corporation   64
27 J.C. Penney Company, Inc.   66
28 J.M. Smuckers Company, Inc. (The)   68
29 JPMorgan Chase & Company   70
30 Kimberly-Clark Corporation   72
31 Lockheed Martin Corporation   74
32 Lowes Companies, Inc.   76
33 Macerich Company (The)   78
34 McDonald's Corporation   80
35 New York Community Bancorp, Inc.   82
36 Newell Rubbermaid, Inc.   84
37 Nike, Inc.   86
38 Philip Morris International, Inc   88
39 Staples, Inc.   90
40 Target Corporation   92
41 Tiffany & Company   94
42 Tyson Foods, Inc.   96
43 United Pacific Corporation   98
44 United Technologies Corporation   100
45 Verizon Communications, Inc.   102
46 Wal-Mart Stores, Inc.   104
47 Waste Management, Inc.   106
48 Weingarten Realty Investors   108
49 Whirlpool Corporation   110
50 Winstream Corporation 112

The Stocks by Index   115
Resources   117
Glossary   119
About the Author   125

Introduction

There is a lot of information on television and the internet about investing and let's face it, most of it is confusing to the average person. This book is written for the independent investor looking for a little straight forward information about investing in stocks. We have all been taught that the stock market is risky and you need thousands of dollars and a financial advisor to invest. Where can an investor turn to buy stocks with smaller dollar amounts? Typically, independent investors will put their money in low risk government bonds, savings accounts and certificates of deposit (CDs); usually these investments produce low returns. Well, there is another option. Dividend stocks have historically produced higher returns than most other investments over the long term. An investor can purchase individual dividend stocks with Direct Stock Purchase Plans (DSPPs); that is buying stocks directly without a broker using small dollar amounts. This is an excellent way to invest in stocks with as little as $50. These investment plans offer a steady way for investors to acquire large amounts of shares over time and are good for the long term investor looking to maximize every dollar.

This book is meant to be a starting point and a guide for investing in stocks. Providing detailed information about DSPPs, such as how to open an account, how often shares are purchased and what fees are charged. This book will also discuss in detail which companies offer the opportunity to start investing with $50. Now, $50 doesn't sound like enough money to start an investment or wealth building plan and most financial advisors would tell you that at least $2,000 is needed.

Introduction

But consider this, $50 invested at 6% every month over 30 years is over $50,000. Investing small amounts can quickly add up over time. Investing in high quality companies with good records of paying consistent dividends, strong financial growth and reinvesting all the dividends into more shares are the keys to building wealth. Buying stock directly from a company can be as easy as opening a bank account. Also, most plans have either no or low fees. The opportunity to invest in companies like McDonalds, Nike and The Coca-Cola Company with investments as small as $50 is made possible with Direct Stock Purchase Plans.

This book also discusses investing in the stock market and explains that investing is not as difficult as the experts in the media would have you believe. Investing based on research and with a proper understanding of the fundamentals of finance are the keys to successful investing.

Investing doesn't have to be complicated, it can even be fun. Remember, you have to invest money to have money; invest $50 today, because your future is your present.

Part I

Getting Started

The Basics of Stock Investing

When some people think of buying stocks, images of Wall Street stockbrokers, confusing terms and endless choices of investments come to mind. Well, it doesn't have to be like that. For the average individual investor the information provided through the media is rarely specific on exactly what to invest in. When there is some advice on a particular stock, the experts will tell you to buy large amounts of shares which usually require a large investment. Depending on the news of the day they may advise you to sell your shares just as quickly. This approach will have you chasing every HOT new stock and never really establishing a solid investment strategy. In order to establish a long term investment strategy an investor has to commit to investing over time. Long term meaning 10 to 25 years, so you do not have to react to every bad day the market may experience. Investing in stocks with Direct Stock Purchase Plans offers the greatest opportunity for the average investor to build wealth over the long term, without investing great amounts of money up front.

What exactly is the Stock Market? In a sentence, it's the buying and selling of companies, no more and no less. The most important thing to remember is buying stock is buying ownership in a company.

A share of stock is simply a piece of ownership in a company and the other shareholders are your partners. If a company has 1 million shares and you own 10,000 shares then you own 1% of the company. As an owner you will benefit when the company makes money in the form of profits. Often the profits are divided amongst the owners in the form of a dividend, usually paid quarterly; the dividend yield is one way to judge the financial health of a company. To calculate the dividend yield take the amount of the dividend and divide it by the price of the stock. For example if Company A is trading at $28.00 per share and they pay a dividend of $1.68 per year, then the dividend yield is 6.00%, ($1.68/$28.00=6%). A dividend is an indicator that the company is profitable enough to reward the investors with a moderate payment. This is one of the ways stocks make money for the investors. The other way is when the shares are sold for a higher price than they were purchased, the difference is the profit. This transaction is called a capital gain. Capital gains and dividends are how investors make money from stocks.

An earnings per share is another indicator of the financial stability of a company. An earnings per share is calculated by dividing the total number of shares outstanding and the total net profit. For example if Company B has 1 Million shares outstanding and has a net profit of $500,000 for the quarter then the company has enough money to pay a $0.25 quarterly dividend (1,000,000/$500,000=$.50). As you can see in this example Company B's profit is more than the dividend payment. Most companies will only pay a portion of the profits in the form of a dividend, leaving the rest for reinvestment back into the business. A company that pays a dividend provides income for the shareholders for each share owned. If you own 100 shares of a company and the quarterly dividend is $0.25 per share then your payment is $25 per quarter. The more shares you own increases your share of the profits.

Which stocks offer solid dividends and dividend growth? Let's face it, finding a company with a guaranteed safe dividend has been a challenge in the last few years. Making good investment decisions can be a difficult task. Choosing a company to invest in should be based on solid information of the financial health of the company.

You must do some homework. Doing your homework is a term that is often used when referring to investing. What does this mean? The simple answer is taking a look at a company that you are familiar with and comfortable with the products or services they provide.

For example, if your favorite sneaker is made by Nike or your favorite soft drink is Coca-Cola, then you might want to study the company as a possible investment. Go to the website of your favorite publicly traded company and then go to the Investor Relations section and read the annual report. The annual report will tell you about the profit or loss the company is experiencing quarterly and annually, the dividend and the earnings per share. It will also explain the company's vision for the future.

It's also important to diversify your portfolio. This useful technique allows investors to spread around the risk they are exposed to. This is important and is at the heart of all successful investment strategies. Investing in different companies over a number of different industries is the practical application of this strategy.

When determining which company is a solid investment you should start with proven leaders and long term winners; companies with a strong history of dividends and growth. A good starting place to find a company to invest is one of the three major Indexes.

Indexes

Dow Jones Industrial Average

The biggest and best stocks are organized in groups called Indexes. The most famous stock index in the United States is the Dow Jones Industrial Average, which is a list of 30 of the largest companies that the entire stock market is measured against. Also known as the Dow 30, most professionals use this index to determine the health of the stock market and the Dow 30 is one of the factors by which the entire U.S. economy is measured. The Dow 30 is the number that is reported on the nightly news, "the Dow was up 100 points or the Dow was down 100 points", the newscaster might say.

What is not said is which of the 30 companies made money that day and which companies lost money. Ultimately, these companies over the long term, not just day to day, have proven to have stability and growth in both dividends and profits.

The 30 companies that make up the Dow 30 include:

3M Co.	*IBM
Alcoa, Inc.	*Intel, Inc.
American Express Co.	Johnson & Johnson
AT&T Inc.	*JP Morgan & Chase & Co.
Boeing Company	Kraft Foods Inc.
Bank of America, Inc	*McDonald's Corp.
*Caterpillar, Inc.	Merck & Co. Inc.
Cisco Systems, Inc.	Microsoft Corp
*Chevron, Inc.	Pfizer, Inc.
*Coca-Cola Company (The)	Procter & Gamble Co.
DuPont & Co.	Travelers Co., Inc. (The)
*Exxon Mobil, Inc.	*United Technologies Corp.
General Electric Co.	*Verizon Commutations, Inc.
Hewlett Packard Co.	Walt Disney Co. (The)
*Home Depot, Inc. (The)	*Wal-Mart Stores, Inc.

The (*) represents the companies that have Direct Stock Purchase Plans, that allow investors to buy shares without a broker and with $50.

Standard & Poor's 500

Another popular index that measures the biggest and best companies in the United States is the Standard & Poor's 500, also known as the S&P 500. The S&P 500 is made up of the 500 biggest companies in the United States based on Market Capitalization. Market Capitalization is the amount of outstanding shares times the share price. For example if Company C has 1 Million shares outstanding and a share price of $28, the Market Capitalization is $28 Million. A list of the S&P 500 companies can be found at www.standardandpoors.com.

Companies in this Index include: McDonalds, Nike and The Coca-Cola Company.

NASDAQ 100

The final major index which measures the largest non-financial and technology companies is the NASDAQ 100. It is also based on Market Capitalization and includes companies incorporated outside of the United States. These factors separate it from the Dow 30 and the exclusion of financial companies separates it from the S&P 500. A list of the NASDAQ 100 companies can be found at www.nasdaq.com. Companies in this Index include: Microsoft, Costco Wholesale and Cisco.

These and many other companies are included on multiple indexes. Also, there are other indexes of stocks in the world of investing compiled by companies like the Standard and Poor's, which measure both industries and the entire market. Membership in these indexes is a strong measurement of the company's strength and longevity. Investing in these indexes through a broker usually comes in the form of an index fund or an exchange traded fund (ETF). However, choosing a group of stocks from these indexes to put in your own portfolio is easy when utilizing Direct Stock Purchase Plans and $50 a month.

Real Estate Investment Trust (REIT)

Another investment option to consider in a wealth building plan is the Real Estate Investment Trust (REIT) sometimes called "real estate stock." In 1960, Congress decided that smaller investors should be able to invest in large-scale, income-producing real estate. It determined that the best way to do this was to follow the investment strategy utilized by other industries by allowing investors to purchase stock.

For many people buying property, particularly commercial buildings, is simply out of reach. The main benefit of the REIT is that you're investing in a group of properties rather than a single building and have less financial risk. They offer the benefits of real estate ownership without the headaches or expense of being a landlord.

Investing in income-generating real estate can be a great way to increase your portfolio value. Pooling your resources with other small investors and investing in large-scale commercial real estate as a group, are the main benefits of REITs.

A company must distribute at least 90 percent of its taxable income to its shareholders each year to qualify as a REIT. There are different categories of REITs, such as office buildings, shopping centers and health care facilities to name a few. Investing in a few of these REITs by buying the stock directly and reinvesting the dividends into more shares can increase the value of your total portfolio. There are 5 REITs, which will be discussed later, that have Direct Stock Purchase Plans that allow investors the opportunity to buy shares with just $50.

Retirement Investing

Investing in Direct Stock Purchase Plans is an excellent way to prepare for retirement. Most people preparing for retirement have a 401k plan, an employer sponsored pension plan or an Individual Retirement Account (IRA). Still, many people don't have any of these. All of us will receive some amount in the form of a U.S. Social Security check however; all of these plans combined may not be enough for a comfortable life after our working days are behind us.

There is no longer guaranteed financial security available to the average person in America. Investing and saving your money on your own, outside of the retirement plan at your job, is the first order of business to a secure financial future. If your investment time is 10 to 30 years, then investing in any of these 50 companies may help you reach your financial or retirement goals.

Part II

Direct Stock Purchase Plans

As the title of the book says, $50 is all you need to start building wealth. Direct Stock Purchase Plans (DSPPs) are plans that provide individual investors the opportunity to buy stock in a company, without the use of a Broker. The key difference between DSPPs and most brokers is brokers will only allow investors to buy shares in whole increments such as 1 to 1,000 shares. But, DSPPs allow individual investors the opportunity to purchase whole or factional shares of stock based on the amount of money they have to invest. Some DSPPs have fees and some allow the investor to invest with no fees or commissions. All of the plans have a minimum amount to start investing which is usually $50-$500; however, all of these plans will **WAIVE** these minimum amounts with consecutive investments of $50 a month or less in some cases. Discipline and constantly putting away money every month is the key to successful investing. This is your opportunity to either begin investing in quality companies or add to your existing investment strategy.

To streamline the investment process and cut down on costs, many companies use an administrator called a Transfer Agent.

Transfer Agents

Whenever you enroll in a Direct Stock Purchase Plan (DSPP) with a publicly traded company, you will conduct all of the transactions involving your investment with a Transfer Agent. Transfer Agents act as an intermediary for the company. The Transfer Agent is responsible for all transactions with new investors and the company. The Transfer Agent will provide each new and existing investor with a prospectus of the company's plan, explaining the plan's details. The role of the Transfer Agent is an important one because publicly traded companies often have many investors who own a small portion of the company. Companies require accurate records and have rights regarding information distribution. Some companies choose to act as their own transfer agent, but most choose from one of a few financial institutions to fill this role.

A Transfer Agent maintains records of investors, account balances and transactions. They also cancel and issue stock certificates, process investor mailings and are responsible for any associated problems. In addition they handle the sale of any shares in the accounts of the shareholders. The selling of shares in a company are sometimes the only fees that the shareholder has to pay, but not always.

The Transfer Agent also collects any fee associated with the administration of the plan and keeps track of the ownership of all the company shares, whether the shares are in stock certificate form or in book-entry form. They will also reinvest dividends into more shares, mail dividend checks or reinvest part of the dividend into more shares and mail the remaining money to the shareholders. In addition, Transfer Agents mail out all investment materials, exchange a company's stock in a merger, handle the shares in an Initial Public Offering (IPO), and mail the company's quarterly and annual reports. And finally, they assist shareholders with questions and any concerns they may have. As you can see, the Transfer Agent plays a vital role with DSPPs.

There are two Transfer Agents which represents most of the Dow 30, S&P 500 and NASDAQ 100 companies, they are:

- **Bank of New York Mellon Corporation**
  www.melloninvestor.com

- **Computershare**
  www.us.computershare.com

Enrolling in Direct Stock Purchase Plans

DSPPs are available to the general public, including company employees and existing shareowners. For new investors to enroll you have to go to the Transfer Agent's website and find the companies you want to invest in. You then decide which account you want to open: an Individual, Joint or Custodial and fill in the necessary information. When enrolling you will have the opportunity to either have the initial $50 debited from a bank account or you can mail a check. At this time you may authorize the necessary number of automatic monthly deductions from your bank account to fund your initial investment. This will purchase whole and fractional shares of the stock; meaning even if the investment is not enough for a share your investment will buy a fractional share up to six decimal points to equal the dollar amount of your investment, less any fees.

If you own shares in a company whose plan you want to participate in and the shares are in a brokerage account, you can have the shares transferred to the Transfer Agent for a small fee or in many cases for free. Just contact the broker and request a Direct Registration System (DRS) transfer and this transaction will establish your account with the Transfer Agent.

If you are an existing registered shareholder of a company, meaning you have stock certificates in your name, you can enroll in the plan by simply going to the Transfer Agent's website and filling out the necessary information or by completing and submitting an enrollment form. All plans may or may not have fees.

Automatic Investing

Automatic investing is a convenient option to get more money invested in the company's stock. A $50 debit from your checking or savings account is invested every 1st or 15th of each month or the next business day if the 1st or 15th is not a business day. The funds will normally be invested within five business days. This steady investment will allow you to avoid the minimum initial amount set by the company and is a great way to purchase more shares using whole dollar amounts.

Dividend Reinvesting

Investing in more shares with dividends is easy. The Transfer Agent will, upon your approval, automatically reinvest dividends into more shares, which will purchase whole and fractional shares of the stock to equal the dollar amount of the dividends, less any fees. You may change your reinvestment instruction through the Internet, by telephone or in writing at any time. If the Transfer Agent receives the notice of change after a dividend payment date, the Transfer Agent may defer changing your reinvestment option until the next dividend payment date.

Selling Shares

You may sell all or a portion of the whole shares of stock in your account at any time either online or by telephone, upon your request by the following methods:

- **Market Order Sale**

    A market order is a request to sell shares promptly at the current market price. Market order sales are only available at the Transfer Agent's website. Each market order sale will incur a transaction fee.

- **Batch Order Sale**

    A batch order is an accumulation of all sales requests from shareholders for a stock submitted together as a collective request. Batch orders are submitted on each weekday, assuming there are sale requests to be processed. Sale instructions for batch orders received by the Transfer Agent will be processed no later than five business days after the date the order is received.

- **Online Sale Requests**

    You can go to the Transfer Agent's website and complete sales request online. Market order and Batch order sales, are available options when selling shares online.

- **Telephone Sale Requests**

    Sale requests can be submitted via telephone to the Transfer Agent. You will be asked to verify your identity by providing specific account information.

- **Sale Requests by Mail**

    You can sell shares by completing and signing the transaction form included with your statement and mail the instructions to the Transfer Agent at the address listed on your statement. All owners registered on the account must sign the transaction form.

Fees

When investing in DSPPs there are some fees associated with the transactions. There are many plans that have no fee to open an account or purchase stock. However, if the company you are interested in has fees the Transfer Agent does its' best to keep them to a minimum.

Statements

The Transfer Agent will mail all transactions and activity in the account to the account holders on a monthly basis. The statement will show the number of shares held by the shareholder, the number of shares for which dividends are being reinvested, any cash received for the purchase of shares, the price per share for any purchases or sales, and any fees for each transaction charged to the shareholder. The shareholders' continuing record of the cost of the purchases and dividends reinvested should be kept for income tax purposes.

Taxes

Taxes are a part of investing that you have to pay attention to. All dividend and capital gains are taxable income. Each company will send out a year-end statement of all dividends on IRS tax form 1099-Div. If a shareholder sells shares in their account, the Transfer Agent will send a Form 1099-B to the shareholders and the IRS showing the total proceeds of the transactions. Please consult a tax professional for all up to date regulations.

Part III

Direct Stock Purchase Plans (DSPPs)

Investing with Just $50

"The most important thing to remember is buying stock is buying ownership in a company."

Aetna, Inc.   1

151 Farmington Avenue
Hartford, Connecticut 06156
(860) 273-0123
Company website: **www.aetna.com**

Company Description

Aetna Inc. is a diversified health care benefits company. Its offers a range of traditional and consumer-directed health insurance products and related services, including medical, pharmacy, dental, behavioral health, group life and disability plans. Aetna's customers include employer groups, individuals, college students, part-time and hourly workers, health plans, governmental units, government-sponsored plans and labor group. It operates under three segments: Health Care, Group Insurance and Large Case Pensions. The Health Care segment provides medical, pharmacy benefits management, dental, behavioral health, and vision plans offered on both an insured basis and an employer-funded basis. Its medical products include point of service, preferred provider organization, health maintenance organization, and indemnity benefit plans, as well as health savings accounts and Aetna Health Fund.

Basic Company Statistics

New York Stock Exchange: **AET**

Industry: **Health Care**

Index Membership: **S&P 500**

Annual Revenue: **$34.76 Billion**

Market Capitalization: **$12.8 Billion (Large-Cap)**

Common Shares Outstanding: **400 Million**

Earnings per Share: **$2.84**

Annual Dividend: **$.04**

Paying Dividends Since: **2001**

Direct Stock Purchase Plan Summary

Transfer Agent: **Computershare**
Transfer Agent website: www-us.computershare.com
Phone: 1-800-446-2617

New Account Investment Options:
One-time minimum purchase by either a check or an authorized one-time deduction from a savings or checking account: **$500.00** or the **$500.00** is waived for a minimum on-going investment of **$50.00** for 10 consecutive months.

Existing Shareholders:
Minimum share required to enroll for existing shareholders: **1**
Optional Cash Purchase Minimum: **$50.00**
Optional Cash Purchase Frequency: **Weekly**
Maximum Annual Investment: **$250,000.00**
Stock Certificate issued upon request: **Yes**
Dividend Frequency: **Annually**

Plan Fees:
Initial Set up Fee: **$5.00**
Cash Purchase Fee: **$5.00**
Cash Purchase-ongoing Fee: **$1.00**
Cash Purchase Processing Fee (per share): **$0.10**
Dividend Reinvestment Fee: **$0.00**
Batch Order Sale: **$15.00**
Batch Order Processing Fee: **$0.10 per share**

How much stock does the first $50 buy? :
Initial Investment: **$50.00**
  Minus Initial Set up Fee: **$5.00**
  Cash Purchase Fee: **$5.00**
  Cash Purchase Processing Fee (per share): **$0.10**
Total Investment: **$39.90**, Sample Stock Price: **$31.02**
Total Shares Purchased: $39.90/$31.02 = **1.286267**

Altria Group, Inc.   2

6601 West Broad Street
Richmond, Virginia 23230
(804) 274-2200
Company website: **www.altria.com**

Company Description

Altria Group, Inc. is a holding company. It primarily offers cigarettes under the Marlboro, Virginia Slims, and Parliament brands; smokeless tobacco products under the Copenhagen, Skoal, Red Seal, and Husky brands and machine-made large cigars and pipe tobacco. The company also maintains a portfolio of leveraged and direct finance leases principally in transportation, including aircraft, as well as power generation and manufacturing equipment and facilities. It serves wholesalers, including distributors; large retail organizations, such as chain stores; and the armed services. As of December 31, 2009, Altria Group, Inc.'s wholly owned subsidiaries included Philip Morris USA Inc., which is engaged in the manufacture and sale of cigarettes and certain smokeless products in the United States.

Basic Company Statistics

New York Stock Exchange: **MO**

Industry: **Tobacco Products**

Index Membership: **S&P 500**

Annual Revenue: **$16.8 Billion**

Market Capitalization: **$51 Billion (Large-Cap)**

Common Shares Outstanding: **2 Billion**

Earnings per Share: **$1.54**

Annual Dividend: **$1.52**

Paying Dividends Since: **1928**

Direct Stock Purchase Plan Summary

Transfer Agent: **Computershare**
Transfer Agent website: www-us.computershare.com
Phone: 1-800-442-0077

New Account Investment Options:
One-time minimum purchase by either a check or an authorized one-time deduction from a savings or checking account: **$500.00** or the **$500.00** is waived for a minimum on-going investment of **$50.00** for 5 consecutive months.

Existing Shareholders:
Minimum share required to enroll for existing shareholders: **1**
Optional Cash Purchase Minimum: **$50.00**
Optional Cash Purchase Frequency: **Weekly**
Maximum Annual Investment: **$250,000.00**
Stock Certificate issued upon request: **Yes**
Dividend Frequency: **Quarterly**

Plan Fees:
Initial Set up Fee: **$10.00**
Cash Purchase Fee: **$5.00**
Cash Purchase-ongoing Fee: **$2.50**
Cash Purchase Processing Fee (per share): **$0.03**
Dividend Reinvestment Fee: **5% of the amount up to $3.00**
Batch Order Sale Fee: **$15.00**
Market Order Sale Fee: **$25.00**
Batch and Market Order Processing Fee: **$0.12 per share**

How much stock does the first $50 buy? :
Initial Investment: **$50.00**
  Minus Initial Set up Fee: **$10.00**
  Cash Purchase Fee: **$5.00**
  Cash Purchase Processing Fee (per share): **$0.03**
Total Investment: **$34.97**, Sample Stock Price: **$22.16**
Total Shares Purchased: $34.97/$22.16 = **1.578069**

American Electric Power Company, Inc.   3

1 Riverside Plaza
Columbus, Ohio 43215
(614) 716-1000
Company website: **www.aep.com**

Company Description

American Electric Power Company, Inc. is a holding company. Its public utility subsidiaries include Appalachian Power Company, Columbus Southern Power Company, Indiana Michigan Power Company, Kentucky Power Company, Kingsport Power Company, Ohio Power Company and Public Service Company of Oklahoma. Also, Southwestern Electric Power Company, Texas Central Company, Texas North Company, Wheeling Power Company and AEP Generating Company. The service areas of AEP's public utility subsidiaries cover portions of the states of Arkansas, Indiana, Kentucky, Louisiana, Michigan, Ohio, Oklahoma, Tennessee, Texas, Virginia and West Virginia. The subsidiaries of AEP provide electric service, consisting of generation, transmission and distribution to their retail customers.

Basic Company Statistics

New York Stock Exchange: **AEP**

Industry: **Electric Utilities**

Index Membership: **S&P 500**

Annual Revenue: **$13.4 Billion**

Market Capitalization: **$17.48 Billion (Large-Cap)**

Common Shares Outstanding: **480 Million**

Earnings per Share: **$2.97**

Annual Dividend: **$1.84**

Paying Dividends Since: **1909**

Direct Stock Purchase Plan Summary

Transfer Agent: **Computershare**
Transfer Agent website: www-us.computershare.com
Phone: 1-800-328-6955

New Account Investment Options:
One-time minimum purchase by either a check or an authorized one-time deduction from a savings or checking account: **$250.00** or the **$250.00** is waived for a minimum on-going investment of **$25.00** for 10 consecutive months.

Existing Shareholders:
Minimum share required to enroll for existing shareholders: **1**
Optional Cash Purchase Minimum: **$25.00**
Optional Cash Purchase Frequency: **Weekly**
Maximum Annual Investment: **$150,000.00**
Stock Certificate issued upon request: **Yes**
Dividend Frequency: **Quarterly**

Plan Fees:
Initial Set up Fee: **$10.00**
Cash Purchase Fee: **$0.00**
Cash Purchase-ongoing Fee: **$0.00**
Cash Purchase Processing Fee (per share): **$0.00**
Dividend Reinvestment Fee: **$0.00**
Batch Order Sale Fee: **$5.00**
Market Order Sale Fee: **$25.00**
Batch and Market Order Processing Fee: **$0.12 per share**

How much stock does the first $50 buy? :
Initial Investment: **$50.00**
  Minus Initial Set up Fee: **$10.00**
  Cash Purchase Fee: **$0.00**
  Cash Purchase Processing Fee (per share): **$0.00**
Total Investment: **$40.00**, Sample Stock Price: **$35.98**
Total Shares Purchased: $40.00/$35.98 = **1.111729**

Aqua America, Inc.   4

762 West Lancaster Avenue
Bryn Mawr, Pennsylvania 19010
(610) 527-8000
Company website: **www.aquaamerica.com**

Company Description

Aqua America, Inc. is the holding company for regulated utilities providing water or wastewater services to approximately three million people in Pennsylvania, Ohio, North Carolina, Illinois, Texas, New Jersey, New York, Florida, Indiana, Virginia, Maine, Missouri, South Carolina and Georgia. The Company's operating subsidiary, Aqua Pennsylvania, Inc., accounted for approximately 52% of its operating revenues for the year ended December 31, 2009. As of December 31, 2009, it provided water or wastewater services and is located in the suburban areas in counties north and west of the City of Philadelphia and in 25 other counties in Pennsylvania. Its other subsidiaries provide similar services in 13 other states. In January 2009, Aqua Pennsylvania, Inc. completed the acquisition of the Gouldsboro Water Company.

Basic Company Statistics

New York Stock Exchange: **WTR**

Industry: **Water Utilities**

Index Membership: **S&P 1500**

Annual Revenue: **$670.5 Million**

Market Capitalization: **$2.8 Billion (Mid-Cap)**

Common Shares Outstanding: **137 Million**

Earnings per Share: **$0.77**

Annual Dividend: **$0.62**

Paying Dividends Since: **1939**

Direct Stock Purchase Plan Summary

Transfer Agent: **Computershare**
Transfer Agent website: www-us.computershare.com
Phone: 1-800-205-8314

New Account Investment Options:
One-time minimum purchase by either a check or an authorized one-time deduction from a savings or checking account: **$500.00** or the **$500.00** is waived for a minimum on-going investment of **$50.00** for 10 consecutive months.

Existing Shareholders:
Minimum shares required to enroll for existing shareholders: **5**
Optional Cash Purchase Minimum: **$50.00**
Optional Cash Purchase Frequency: **Weekly**
Maximum Annual Investment: **$250,000.00**
Stock Certificate issued upon request: **Yes**
Dividend Frequency: **Quarterly**

Plan Fees:
Initial Set up Fee: **$0.00**
Cash Purchase Fee: **$0.00**
Cash Purchase-ongoing Fee: **$0.00**
Cash Purchase Processing Fee (per share): **$0.00**
Dividend Reinvestment Fee: **$0.00**
Batch Order Sale Fee: **$15.00**
Market Order Sale Fee: **$25.00**
Batch and Market Order Processing Fee: **$0.15 per share**

How much stock does the first $50 buy? :
Initial Investment: **$50.00**
  Minus Initial Set up Fee: **$0.00**
  Cash Purchase Fee: **$0.00**
  Cash Purchase Processing Fee (per share): **$0.00**
Total Investment: **$50.00**, Sample Stock Price: **$19.49**
Total Shares Purchased: $50.00/$19.49 = **2.565418**

Bank of South Carolina Corporation 5

256 Meeting Street
Charleston, South Carolina 29401
(843) 724-1500
Company website: **www.banksc.com**

Company Description

Bank of South Carolina Corporation is a bank holding company that operates, through its wholly owned subsidiary, The Bank of South Carolina. The Bank is a state-chartered financial institution. The Bank serves Berkeley, Charleston and Dorchester counties. The Bank offers a range of deposit services. The lending services offered by the Bank include a range of commercial, personal and mortgage loans. Its primary focus is on business lending. Other services offered, but not limited to, include safe deposit boxes, letters of credit, travelers checks, direct deposit of payroll, social security and dividend payments, and automatic payment of insurance premiums and mortgage loans.

Basic Company Statistics

NASDAQ: **BKSC**

Industry: **Banking**

Index Membership: **None**

Annual Revenue: **$13.94 Million**

Market Capitalization: **$47 Million (Small-Cap)**

Common Shares Outstanding: **4 Million**

Earnings per Share: **$0.43**

Annual Dividend: **$0.40**

Paying Dividends Since: **1986**

Direct Stock Purchase Plan Summary

Transfer Agent: **Computershare**
Transfer Agent website: www-us.computershare.com
Phone: 1-781-575-2879

New Account Investment Options:
One-time minimum purchase by either a check or an authorized one-time deduction from a savings or checking account: **$250.00** or the **$250.00** is waived for a minimum on-going investment of **$50.00** for 5 consecutive months.

Existing Shareholders:
Minimum share required to enroll for existing shareholders: **1**
Optional Cash Purchase Minimum: **$50.00**
Optional Cash Purchase Frequency: **Weekly**
Maximum Annual Investment: **$250,000.00**
Stock Certificate issued upon request: **Yes**
Dividend Frequency: **Quarterly**

Plan Fees:
Initial Set up Fee: **$5.00**
Cash Purchase Fee: **$5.00**
Cash Purchase-ongoing Fee: **$2.50**
Cash Purchase Processing Fee (per share): **$0.10**
Dividend Reinvestment Fee: **5% of the amount up to $3.00**
Batch Order Sale Fee: **$15.00**
Batch Processing Fee: **$0.10 per share**

How much stock does the first $50 buy? :
Initial Investment: **$50.00**
  Minus Initial Set up Fee: **$5.00**
  Cash Purchase Fee: **$5.00**
  Cash Purchase Processing Fee (per share): **$0.10**
Total Investment: **$39.90**, Sample Stock Price: **$11.75**
Total Shares Purchased: $39.90/$11.75 = **3.395745**

Becton, Dickinson and Company 6

1 Becton Drive
Franklin Lakes, New Jersey 07417
(201) 847-6800
Company website: www.bd.com

Company Description

Becton, Dickinson and Company is a medical technology company engaged principally in the development, manufacture and sale of a range of medical supplies, devices, instrument systems and reagents used by healthcare institutions, life science researchers, clinical laboratories, the pharmaceutical industry and the general public. BD's operations consist of three business segments: BD Medical, BD Diagnostics and BD Biosciences. On November 19, 2009, BD acquired 100% of HandyLab, Inc. a company that develops and manufactures molecular diagnostic assays and automation platforms.

Basic Company Statistics

New York Stock Exchange: **BDX**

Industry: **Health Care Equipment**

Index Membership: **S&P 500**

Annual Revenue: **$7.1 Billion**

Market Capitalization: **$17.7 Billion (Large-Cap)**

Common Shares Outstanding: **232 Million**

Earnings per Share: **$4.92**

Annual Dividend: **$1.48**

Paying Dividends Since: **1926**

Direct Stock Purchase Plan Summary

Transfer Agent: **Computershare**
Transfer Agent website: www-us.computershare.com
Phone: 1-781-575-2879

New Account Investment Options:
One-time minimum purchase by either a check or an authorized one-time deduction from a savings or checking account: **$250.00** or the **$250.00** is waived for a minimum on-going investment of **$50.00** for 5 consecutive months.

Existing Shareholders:
Minimum share required to enroll for existing shareholders: **1**
Optional Cash Purchase Minimum: **$50.00**
Optional Cash Purchase Frequency: **Weekly**
Maximum Annual Investment: **$99,999,999.00**
Stock Certificate issued upon request: **Yes**
Dividend Frequency: **Quarterly**

Plan Fees:
Initial Set up Fee: **$0.00**
Cash Purchase Fee: **$0.00**
Cash Purchase-ongoing Fee: **$0.00**
Cash Purchase Processing Fee (per share): **$0.00**
Dividend Reinvestment Fee: **$0.00**
Batch Order Sale Fee: **$15.00**
Batch Processing Fee: **$0.12 per share**

How much stock does the first $50 buy? :
Initial Investment: **$50.00**
  Minus Initial Set up Fee: **$0.00**
  Cash Purchase Fee: **$0.00**
  Cash Purchase Processing Fee (per share): **$0.00**
Total Investment: $50.00, Sample Stock Price: **$75.52**
Total Shares Purchased: $50.00/$75.52 = .662076

Best Buy Company, Inc. 7

7601 Penn Avenue South
Richfield, Minnesota 55423
(612) 291-1000
Company website: www.bestbuy.com

Company Description

Best Buy Co., Inc. is a multinational retailer of consumer electronics, home office products, entertainment software, appliances and related services. It operates in two segments: Domestic and International. The Domestic segment consists of the operations in all states, districts and territories of the United States, operating under various brand names, including, Best Buy, Best Buy Mobile, Geek Squad, Magnolia Audio Video, Napster, Pacific Sales and Speakeasy. The International segment consists of all Canadian operations, operating under the brand names Best Buy, Best Buy Mobile, Future Shop and Geek Squad; all Europe operations, operating under the brand names The Carphone Warehouse, The Phone House and Geek Squad; all China operations, operating under the brand names Best Buy, Geek Squad and Five Star.

Basic Company Statistics

New York Stock Exchange: **BBY**

Industry: **Retail**

Index Membership: **S&P 500**

Annual Revenue: **$49.69 Billion**

Market Capitalization: **$17.1 Billion (Large-Cap)**

Common Shares Outstanding: **397 Million**

Earnings per Share: **$2.39**

Annual Dividend: **$0.60**

Paying Dividends Since: **2003**

Direct Stock Purchase Plan Summary

Transfer Agent: **Computershare**
Transfer Agent website: www-us.computershare.com
Phone: 1-781-575-2879

New Account Investment Options:
One-time minimum purchase by either a check or an authorized one-time deduction from a savings or checking account: **$500.00** or the **$500.00** is waived for a minimum on-going investment of **$50.00** for 10 consecutive months.

Existing Shareholders:
Minimum share required to enroll for existing shareholders: **1**
Optional Cash Purchase Minimum: **$50.00**
Optional Cash Purchase Frequency: **Weekly**
Maximum Annual Investment: **$250,000.00**
Stock Certificate issued upon request: **Yes**
Dividend Frequency: **Quarterly**

Plan Fees:
Initial Set up Fee: **$10.00**
Cash Purchase Fee: **$5.00**
Cash Purchase-ongoing Fee: **$2.50**
Cash Purchase Processing Fee (per share): **$0.03**
Dividend Reinvestment Fee: **5% of the amount up to $3.00**
Batch Order Sale Fee: **$15.00**
Batch Processing Fee: **$0.12 per share**

How much stock does the first $50 buy? :
Initial Investment: **$50.00**
  Minus Initial Set up Fee: **$10.00**
  Cash Purchase Fee: **$5.00**
  Cash Purchase Processing Fee (per share): **$0.03**
Total Investment: **$34.97**, Sample Stock Price: **$42.98**
Total Shares Purchased: $34.97/$42.98 = **.813634**

Campbell Soup Company   8

One Campbell Place
Camden, New Jersey 08103
(856) 342-4800
Company website: **www.campbellsoupcompany.com**

Company Description

Campbell Soup Company, together with its subsidiaries, engages in the manufacture and marketing of branded convenience food products worldwide. The company operates through four segments: U.S. Soup, Sauces, and Beverages; Baking and Snacking; International Soup, Sauces, and Beverages; and North America Foodservice. The U.S. Soup, Sauces, and Beverages segment offers condensed and ready-to-serve soups; broth, stocks, and canned poultry; pasta sauce; Mexican sauce; canned pasta, gravies, and beans; juice and juice drinks; tomato juice; and soups. The Baking and Snacking segment provides cookies, crackers, and bakery and frozen products in the United States retail, and Arnott's biscuits in Australia and Asia Pacific. The International Soup, Sauces and Beverages segment includes the soup, sauce and beverage businesses outside of the United States. The North America Foodservice segment includes the Company's Away From Home operations.

Basic Company Statistics

New York Stock Exchange: **CPB**

Industry: **Processed & Packaged Goods**

Index Membership: **S&P 500**

Annual Revenue: **$7.5 Billion**

Market Capitalization: **$12.1 Billion (Large-Cap)**

Common Shares Outstanding: **336 Million**

Earnings per Share: **$2.04**

Annual Dividend: **$1.10**

Paying Dividends Since: **1902**

Direct Stock Purchase Plan Summary

Transfer Agent: **Computershare**
Transfer Agent website: www-us.computershare.com
Phone: 1-800-780-3203

New Account Investment Options:
One-time minimum purchase by either a check or an authorized one-time deduction from a savings or checking account: **$500.00** or the **$500.00** is waived for a minimum on-going investment of **$50.00** for 10 consecutive months.

Existing Shareholders:
Minimum share required to enroll for existing shareholders: **1**
Optional Cash Purchase Minimum: **$50.00**
Optional Cash Purchase Frequency: **Weekly**
Maximum Annual Investment: **$350,000.00**
Stock Certificate issued upon request: **Yes**
Dividend Frequency: **Quarterly**

Plan Fees:
Initial Set up Fee: **$15.00**
Cash Purchase Fee: **$5.00**
Cash Purchase-ongoing Fee: **$2.00**
Cash Purchase Processing Fee (per share): **$0.03**
Dividend Reinvestment Fee: **5% of the amount up to $3.00**
Batch Order Sale Fee: **$15.00**
Market Order Sale Fee: **$25.00**
Batch and Market Order Processing Fee: **$0.12 per share**

How much stock does the first $50 buy? :
Initial Investment: **$50.00**
  Minus Initial Set up Fee: **$15.00**
  Cash Purchase Fee: **$5.00**
  Cash Purchase Processing Fee (per share): **$0.03**
Total Investment: **$29.97**, Sample Stock Price: **$36.02**
Total Shares Purchased: $29.97/$36.02 = **.832038**

Caterpillar, Inc. 9

100 N.E. Adams Street
Peoria, Illinois 61629
(309) 675-1000
Company website: **www.cat.com**

Company Description

Caterpillar Inc. provides construction and mining equipment, diesel and natural gas engines, and industrial gas turbines. The company is a leader in the industry and operates primarily through three lines of business: Machinery, Engines and Financial Products. Machinery includes the design, manufacture, marketing and sales of construction, mining and forestry machinery. Engines line of business includes the design, manufacture, marketing and sales of engines for Caterpillar machinery, electric power generation systems, locomotives, marine, petroleum, and construction, industrial, agricultural and other applications and related parts.

Basic Company Statistics

New York Stock Exchange: **CAT**

Industry: **Construction Machinery**

Index Memberships: **Dow 30, S&P 500**

Annual Revenue: **$32.39 Billion**

Market Capitalization: **$50.6 Billion (Large-Cap)**

Common Shares Outstanding: **630 Million**

Earnings per Share: **$4.00**

Annual Dividend: **$1.76**

Paying Dividends Since: **1914**

Direct Stock Purchase Plan Summary

Transfer Agent: **Bank of New York Mellon**
Transfer Agent website: www.melloninvestor.com
Phone: 1-866-203-6622

New Account Investment Options:
One-time minimum purchase by either a check or an authorized one-time deduction from a savings or checking account: **$250.00** or the **$250.00** is waived for a minimum on-going investment of **$25.00** for 10 consecutive months.

Existing Shareholders:
Minimum share required to enroll for existing shareholders: **1**
Optional Cash Purchase Minimum: **$25.00**
Optional Cash Purchase Frequency: **Weekly**
Maximum One Time Investment: **$10,000.00**
Stock Certificate issued upon request: **Yes**
Dividend Frequency: **Quarterly**

Plan Fees:
Initial Set up Fee: **$15.00**
Cash Purchase Fee via check: **$2.50**
Cash Purchase Fee via automatic debit: **$1.00**
Cash Purchase Processing Fee (per share): **$0.03**
Dividend Reinvestment Fee: **5% of the amount up to $3.00**
Market Order Sale: **$15.00**
Market Order Processing Fee: **$0.12 per share**

How much stock does the first $50 buy? :
Initial Investment: **$50.00**
  Minus Initial Set up Fee: **$15.00**
  Cash Purchase Fee via automatic debit: **$1.00**
  Cash Purchase Processing Fee (per share): **$0.03**
Total Investment: **$33.97**, Sample Stock Price: **$78.55**
Total Shares Purchased: $33.97/$78.55 = **.4325**

Chemical Financial Corporation   10

235 East Main Street
Midland, Michigan 48640
(989) 839-5350
Company website: www.chemicalbankmi.com

Company Description

Chemical Financial Corporation operates as the holding company for Chemical Bank which offers commercial banking services in Michigan. Its products and services include business and personal checking accounts, savings and individual retirement accounts, time deposit instruments, electronically accessed banking products, residential and commercial real estate financing, commercial lending, consumer financing, debit cards, safe deposit box services, money transfer services, and automated teller machines. The company also provides mutual funds, annuity products, and market securities to customers, as well as issues title insurance to buyers and sellers of residential and commercial mortgage properties, including properties subject to loan refinancing. In addition, it offers corporate and personal trust and investment management services. As of February 23, 2010, the company operated 129 banking offices.

Basic Company Statistics

NASDAQ: **CHFC**

Industry: **Banking**

Index Membership: **None**

Annual Revenue: **$233.9 Million**

Market Capitalization: **$556 Million (Small-Cap)**

Common Shares Outstanding: **27.4 Million**

Earnings per Share: **$0.71**

Annual Dividend: **$0.80**

Paying Dividends Since: **1973**

Direct Stock Purchase Plan Summary

Transfer Agent: **Computershare**
Transfer Agent website: www-us.computershare.com
Phone: 1-800-261-0598

New Account Investment Options:
One-time minimum purchase by either a check or an authorized one-time deduction from a savings or checking account: **$50.00**.

Existing Shareholders:
Minimum share required to enroll for existing shareholders: **1**
Optional Cash Purchase Minimum: **$50.00**
Optional Cash Purchase Frequency: **Weekly**
Maximum Annual Investment: **$40,000.00**
Stock Certificate issued upon request: **Yes**
Dividend Frequency: **Quarterly**

Plan Fees:
Initial Set up Fee: **$0.00**
Cash Purchase Fee: **$0.00**
Cash Purchase-ongoing Fee: **$0.00**
Cash Purchase Processing Fee (per share): **$0.00**
Dividend Reinvestment Fee: **$0.00**
Batch Order Sale Fee: **$12.50**
Batch Processing Fee: **$0.07 per share**

How much stock does the first $50 buy? :
Initial Investment: **$50.00**
  Minus Initial Set up Fee: **$0.00**
  Cash Purchase Fee: **$0.00**
  Cash Purchase Processing Fee (per share): **$0.00**
Total Investment: **$50.00**, Sample Stock Price: **$20.28**
Total Shares Purchased: $50.00/$20.28 = **2.465483**

CH Energy Group, Inc.   11

284 South Avenue
Poughkeepsie, New York 12601
(845) 452-2000
Company website: **www.chenergygroup.com**

Company Description

CH Energy Group, Inc., through its subsidiaries, Central Hudson Gas & Electric Corporation and Central Hudson Enterprises Corporation engages in the electric utility, natural gas utility, and fuel distribution business. Central Hudson purchases, sells at wholesale, and distributes electricity and natural gas at retail in portions of New York State. As of December 31, 2009, it delivered electricity and natural gas to approximately 300,000 electric customers and 74,000 natural gas customers in the Mid-Hudson Valley region of New York State.

Basic Company Statistics

New York Stock Exchange: **CHG**

Industry: **Multi-Utilities**

Index Membership: **S&P 1500**

Annual Revenue: **$931 Million**

Market Capitalization: **$711 Million (Small-Cap)**

Common Shares Outstanding: **15.8 Million**

Earnings per Share: **$2.22**

Annual Dividend: **$2.16**

Paying Dividends Since: **1903**

Direct Stock Purchase Plan Summary

Transfer Agent: **Computershare**
Transfer Agent website: www-us.computershare.com
Phone: 1-800-428-9578

New Account Investment Options:
One-time minimum purchase of either a check or an authorized one-time deduction from a savings or checking account: **$100.00** or the **$100.00** is waived for a minimum on-going investment of **$50.00** for 2 consecutive months.

Existing Shareholders:
Minimum share required to enroll for existing shareholders: **1**
Optional Cash Purchase Minimum: **$50.00**
Optional Cash Purchase Frequency: **Weekly**
Maximum Annual Investment: **$150,000.00**
Stock Certificate issued upon request: **Yes**
Dividend Frequency: **Quarterly**

Plan Fees:
Initial Set up Fee: **$0.00**
Cash Purchase Fee: **$0.00**
Cash Purchase-ongoing Fee: **$0.00**
Cash Purchase Processing Fee (per share): **$0.00**
Dividend Reinvestment Fee: **$0.00**
Batch Order Sale Fee: **$15.00**
Market Order Sale: **$25.00**
Batch and Market Order Processing Fee: **$0.12 per share**

How much stock does the first $50 buy? :
Initial Investment: **$50.00**
  Minus Initial Set up Fee: **$0.00**
  Cash Purchase Fee: **$0.00**
  Cash Purchase Processing Fee (per share): **$0.00**
Total Investment: **$50.00**, Sample Stock Price: **$45.45**
Total Shares Purchased: $50.00/$45.45 = **1.10011**

Chevron Corporation 12

6001 Bollinger Canyon Road
San Ramon, California 94583
(925) 842-1000
Company website: **www.chevron.com**

Company Description

Chevron Corporation manages its investments in subsidiaries and affiliates, and provides administrative, financial, management and technology support to United States and international subsidiaries that engage in fully integrated petroleum operations, chemicals operations, mining operations, power generation and energy services. Exploration and production (upstream) operations consist of exploring for, developing and producing crude oil and natural gas, and also marketing natural gas. Refining, marketing and transportation (downstream) operations relate to refining crude oil and converting natural gas into finished petroleum products; marketing crude oil and the many products derived from petroleum, and transporting crude oil, natural gas and petroleum products by pipeline, marine vessel, motor equipment and rail car.

Basic Company Statistics

New York Stock Exchange: **CVX**

Industry: **Oil & Gas**

Index Memberships: **Dow 30, S&P 500**

Annual Revenue: **$167.4 Billion**

Market Capitalization: **$168 Billion (Large-Cap)**

Common Shares Outstanding: **2 Billion**

Earnings per Share: **$5.24**

Annual Dividend: **$2.88**

Paying Dividends Since: **1912**

Direct Stock Purchase Plan Summary

Transfer Agent: **Bank of New York Mellon**
Transfer Agent website: www.melloninvestor.com
Phone: 1-800-368-8357

New Account Investment Options:
One-time minimum purchase by either a check or an authorized one-time deduction from a savings or checking account: **$250.00** or the **$250.00** is waived for a minimum on-going investment of **$50.00** for 5 consecutive months.

Existing Shareholders:
Minimum share required to enroll for existing shareholders: **1**
Optional Cash Purchase Minimum: **$50.00**
Optional Cash Purchase Frequency: **Weekly**
Maximum One Time Investment: **$100,000.00**
Stock Certificate issued upon request: **Yes**
Dividend Frequency: **Quarterly**

Plan Fees:
Initial Set up Fee: **$10.00**
Cash Purchase Fee via check: **$4.00**
Cash Purchase Fee via automatic debit Fee: **$2.00**
Cash Purchase Processing Fee (per share): **$0.05**
Dividend Reinvestment Fee: **5% of the amount up to $3.00**
Market Order Sale of Shares: **$15.00**
Market Order Processing Fee: **$0.10 per share**

How much stock does the first $50 buy? :
Initial Investment: **$50.00**
  Minus Initial Set up Fee: **$10.00**
  Cash Purchase Fee via automatic debit: **$2.00**
  Cash Purchase Processing Fee (per share): **$0.03**
Total Investment: **$37.97**, Sample Stock Price: **$82.60**
Total Shares Purchased: $37.97/$82.60 = **.4597**

Clorox Company (The)   13

1221 Broadway
Oakland, California 94612
(510) 271-7000
Company website: www.thecloroxcompany.com

Company Description

The Clorox Company is a manufacturer and marketer of consumer and institutional products. The Company sells its products primarily through mass merchandisers, grocery stores and other retail outlets. It markets some brand names, including its namesake bleach and cleaning products, Green Works natural cleaning and laundry products, Poett and Mistolin cleaning products, Armor All and STP auto-care products, Fresh Step and Scoop Away cat litter, Kingsford charcoal, Hidden Valley and K C Masterpiece dressings and sauces, Brita water-filtration systems, Glad bags, wraps and containers, and Burt's Bees natural personal care products.

Basic Company Statistics

New York Stock Exchange: **CLX**

Industry: **Household Products**

Index Membership: **S&P 500**

Annual Revenue: **$5.45 Billion**

Market Capitalization: **$9.44 Billion (Mid-Cap)**

Common Shares Outstanding: **139.3 Million**

Earnings per Share: **$3.81**

Annual Dividend: **$2.20**

Paying Dividends Since: **1968**

Direct Stock Purchase Plan Summary

Transfer Agent: **Computershare**
Transfer Agent website: www-us.computershare.com
Phone: 1-781-575-2726

New Account Investment Options:
One-time minimum purchase by either a check or an authorized one-time deduction from a savings or checking account: **$250.00** or the **$250.00** is waived for a minimum on-going investment of **$50.00** for 5 consecutive months.

Existing Shareholders:
Minimum share required to enroll for existing shareholders: **1**
Optional Cash Purchase Minimum: **$50.00**
Optional Cash Purchase Frequency: **Weekly**
Maximum Annual Investment: **$250,000.00**
Stock Certificate issued upon request: **Yes**
Dividend Frequency: **Quarterly**

Plan Fees:
Initial Set up Fee: **$15.00**
Cash Purchase Fee: **$5.00**
Cash Purchase-ongoing Fee: **$0.00**
Cash Purchase Processing Fee (per share): **$0.03**
Dividend Reinvestment Fee: **$0.00**
Batch Order Sale Fee: **$15.00**
Market Order Sale: **$25.00**
Batch and Market Order Processing Fee: **$0.12 per share**

How much stock does the first $50 buy? :
Initial Investment: **$50.00**
  Minus Initial Set up Fee: **$15.00**
  Cash Purchase Fee: **$5.00**
  Cash Purchase Processing Fee (per share): **$0.03**
Total Investment: **$29.97**, Sample Stock Price: **$68.19**
Total Shares Purchased: $29.97/$68.19 = **0.439507**

Coca Cola Company (The)   14

One Coca-Cola Plaza
Atlanta, Georgia 94583
(404) 676-2121
Company website: www.thecoca-colacompany.com

Company Description

The Coca-Cola Company is the owner and marketer of nonalcoholic beverage brands. It also manufactures, distributes and markets concentrates and syrups used to produce nonalcoholic beverages. The company owns or licenses and markets more than 500 nonalcoholic beverage brands, primarily sparkling beverages but also a variety of still beverages, such as waters, enhanced waters, juices and juice drinks, ready-to-drink teas and coffees, and energy and sports drinks. It also manufactures, or authorizes bottling partners to manufacture, fountain syrups, which it sells to fountain retailers, such as restaurants and convenience stores, which use the fountain syrups to produce finished beverages for immediate consumption, or to fountain wholesalers or bottlers, which in turn sell and distribute the fountain syrups to fountain retailers. In addition, the company manufactures certain finished beverages, such as juices and juice drinks and water products.

Basic Company Statistics

New York Stock Exchange: **KO**

Industry: **Beverages**

Index Memberships: **Dow Jones 30, S&P 500**

Annual Revenue: **$30.99 Billion**

Market Capitalization: **$138.4 Billion (Large-Cap)**

Common Shares Outstanding: **2.30 Billion**

Earnings per Share: **$2.93**

Annual Dividend: **$1.76**

Paying Dividends Since: **1893**

Direct Stock Purchase Plan Summary

Transfer Agent: **Computershare**
Transfer Agent website: www-us.computershare.com
Phone: 1-888-265-3747

New Account Investment Options:
One-time minimum purchase by either a check or an authorized one-time deduction from a savings or checking account: **$500.00** or the **$500.00** is waived for a minimum on-going investment of **$50.00** for 10 consecutive months.

Existing Shareholders:
Minimum share required to enroll for existing shareholders: **1**
Optional Cash Purchase Minimum: **$50.00**
Optional Cash Purchase Frequency: **Weekly**
Maximum One Time Investment: **$250,000.00 per year**
Stock Certificate issued upon request: **Yes**
Dividend Frequency: **Quarterly**

Plan Fees:
Initial Set up Fee: **$10.00**
Cash Purchase Fee: **$3.00**
On-going Automatic Investment Fee: **$2.00**
Cash Purchase Processing Fee (per share): **$0.03**
Dividend Reinvestment Fee: **5% up to a maximum of $2.00**
Batch Order Sale Fee: **$15.00**
Market Order Sale Fee: **$25.00**
Batch and Market Order Processing Fee: **$0.12 per share**

How much stock does the first $50 buy? :
Initial Investment: **$50.00**
  Minus Initial Set up Fee: **$10.00**
  Cash Purchase Fee: **$3.00**
  Cash Purchase Processing Fee (per share): **$0.03**
Total Investment: **$36.97**, Sample Stock Price: **$61.32**
Total Shares Purchased: $36.97/$61.32 = **.602903**

Colonial Properties Trust   15

2101 6th Avenue North
Suite 750
Birmingham, Alabama 35203
(205) 250-8700
Company website: **www.colonialprop.com**

Company Description

Colonial Properties Trust is a real estate investment trust (REIT). The firm engages in the acquisition, development, ownership, management, and leasing of commercial real estate properties. It invests in the public equity and real estate markets of the United States. The firm primarily invests in multifamily, office, retail, and for-sale properties. It develops mixed-use communities and merchant build properties. Colonial Properties Trust was founded on July 9, 1993 and is headquartered in Birmingham, Alabama.

Basic Company Statistics

New York Stock Exchange: **CLP**

Industry: **REIT - Residential**

Index Membership: **S&P 1500**

Annual Revenue: **$339.1 Million**

Market Capitalization: **$1.4 Billion (Small-Cap)**

Common Shares Outstanding: **71.2 Million**

Earnings per Share: **$2.42**

Annual Dividend: **$0.60**

Paying Dividends Since: **1994**

Direct Stock Purchase Plan Summary

Transfer Agent: **Computershare**
Transfer Agent website: www-us.computershare.com
Phone: 1-866-897-1807

New Account Investment Options:
One-time minimum purchase by either a check or an authorized one-time deduction from a savings or checking account: **$200.00** or the **$200.00** is waived for a minimum on-going investment of **$25.00** for 8 consecutive months.

Existing Shareholders:
Minimum share required to enroll for existing shareholders: **1**
Optional Cash Purchase Minimum: **$25.00**
Optional Cash Purchase Frequency: **Weekly**
Maximum One Time Investment: **$90,000 per year**
Stock Certificate issued upon request: **Yes**
Dividend Frequency: **Quarterly**

Plan Fees:
Initial Set up Fee: **$0.00**
Cash Purchase Fee: **$0.00**
On-going Automatic Investment Fee: **$0.00**
Cash Purchase Processing Fee (per share): **$0.03**
Dividend Reinvestment Fee: **$0.00**
Batch Order Sale Fee: **$15.00**
Batch Order Processing Fee: **$0.12 per share**

How much stock does the first $50 buy? :
Initial Investment: **$50.00**
  Minus Initial Set up Fee: **$0.00**
  Cash Purchase Fee: **$0.00**
  Cash Purchase Processing Fee (per share): **$0.03**
Total Investment: **$49.97**, Sample Stock Price: **$17.93**
Total Shares Purchased: $49.97/$17.93 = **2.786949**

ConocoPhillips 16

600 North Dairy Ashford
Houston, Texas 77079
(281) 293-1000
Company website: **www.conocophillips.com**

Company Description

ConocoPhillips is an international, integrated energy company. It has six segments. Its E&P segment explores produces, transports and markets crude oil, natural gas, natural gas liquids and bitumen on a worldwide basis. The Midstream segment gathers, processes and markets natural gas produced by ConocoPhillips and others, and fractionates and markets natural gas liquids, predominantly in the United States and Trinidad. Its R&M segment purchases, refines, markets and transports crude oil and petroleum products. The Lukoil Investment segment consists of its equity investment in the common shares of Lukoil.

Basic Company Statistics

New York Stock Exchange: **COP**

Industry: **Oil & Gas**

Index Membership: **S&P 500**

Annual Revenue: **$149.3 Billion**

Market Capitalization: **$90.1 Billion (Large-Cap)**

Common Shares Outstanding: **1.43 Billion**

Earnings per Share: **$3.24**

Annual Dividend: **$2.20**

Paying Dividends Since: **1934**

Direct Stock Purchase Plan Summary

Transfer Agent: **Bank of New York Mellon**
Transfer Agent website: www.melloninvestor.com
Phone: 1-800-356-0066

New Account Investment Options:
One-time minimum purchase by either a check or an authorized one-time deduction from a savings or checking account: **$250.00** or the **$250.00** is waived for a minimum on-going investment of **$25.00** for 10 consecutive months.

Existing Shareholders:
Minimum share required to enroll for existing shareholders: **1**
Optional Cash Purchase Minimum: **$25.00**
Optional Cash Purchase Frequency: **Weekly**
Maximum One Time Investment: **$120,000.00**
Stock Certificate issued upon request: **Yes**
Dividend Frequency: **Quarterly**

Plan Fees:
Initial Set up Fee: **$0.00**
Cash Purchase Fee via check: **$0.00**
Cash Purchase Fee via automatic debit: **$0.00**
Cash Purchase Processing Fee (per share): **$0.00**
Dividend Reinvestment Fee: **$0.00**
Batch Order Sale Fee: **$15.00**
Batch Order Processing Fee: **$0.05 per share**

How much stock does the first $50 buy? :
Initial Investment: **$50.00**
  Minus Initial Set up Fee: **$0.00**
  Cash Purchase Fee via automatic debit: **$0.00**
  Cash Purchase Processing Fee (per share): **$0.00**
Total Investment: **$50.00**, Sample Stock Price: **$61.67**
Total Shares Purchased: $50.00/$61.67 = **.8108**

Costco Wholesale Corporation 17

999 Lake Drive
Issaquah, Washington 98027
(425) 313-8100
Company website: **www.costco.com**

Company Description

Costco Wholesale Corporation operates membership warehouses that offer its member's low prices on a limited selection of branded and selected private-label products in a range of merchandise categories. It buys the majority of its merchandise directly from manufacturers and routes it to a cross-docking consolidation point or directly to its warehouses. The Company's depots receive container-based shipments from manufacturers and reallocate these goods for shipment to its individual warehouses. The Company's warehouse format averages approximately 143,000 square feet. Its warehouses operate on a seven-day, 69-hour week.

Basic Company Statistics

NASDAQ: **COST**

Industry: **Retail**

Index Memberships: **S&P 500, NASDAQ 100**

Annual Revenue: **$71.4 Billion**

Market Capitalization: **$27.97 Billion (Large-Cap)**

Common Shares Outstanding: **439.1 Million**

Earnings per Share: **$2.47**

Annual Dividend: **$0.82**

Paying Dividends Since: **2004**

Direct Stock Purchase Plan Summary

Transfer Agent: **Bank of New York Mellon**
Transfer Agent website: www.melloninvestor.com
Phone: 1-800-249-8982

New Account Investment Options:
One-time minimum purchase by either a check or an authorized one-time deduction from a savings or checking account: **$250.00** or the **$250.00** is waived for a minimum on-going investment of **$25.00** for 10 consecutive months.

Existing Shareholders:
Minimum share required to enroll for existing shareholders: **1**
Optional Cash Purchase Minimum: **$25.00**
Optional Cash Purchase Frequency: **Weekly**
Maximum One Time Investment: **$10,000.00**
Stock Certificate issued upon request: **Yes**
Dividend Frequency: **Quarterly**

Plan Fees:
Initial Set up Fee: **$15.00**
Cash Purchase Fee via check: **$5.00**
Cash Purchase Fee via automatic debit: **$2.00**
Cash Purchase Processing Fee (per share): **$0.03**
Dividend Reinvestment Fee: **5% of the amount up to $3.00**
Market Order Sale Fee: **$15.00**
Market Order Processing Fee: **$0.12 per share**

How much stock does the first $50 buy? :
Initial Investment: **$50.00**
  Minus Initial Set up Fee: **$15.00**
  Cash Purchase Fee via automatic debit: **$2.00**
  Cash Purchase Processing Fee (per share): **$0.03**
Total Investment: **$32.97**, Sample Stock Price: **$64.03**
Total Shares Purchased: $32.97/$64.03 = **.5149**

Dr. Pepper Snapple Group, Inc.   18

5301 Legacy Drive
Plano, Texas 75024
(972) 673-7000
Company website: **www.drpeppersnapplegroup.com**

Company Description

Dr Pepper Snapple Group, Inc. is an integrated brand owner, manufacturer and distributor of non-alcoholic beverages in the United States, Canada and Mexico with a varied portfolio of flavored (non-cola) carbonated soft drinks (CSD) and non-carbonated beverages (NCB), including ready-to-drink teas, juices, juice drinks and mixers. DPS has three segments: Beverage Concentrates, Packaged Beverages and Latin America Beverages. The Company's brand portfolio includes Dr Pepper, Sunkist soda, 7UP, A&W, and Canada Dry.

Basic Company Statistics

New York Stock Exchange: **DPS**

Industry: **Beverages**

Index Membership: **S&P 500**

Annual Revenue: **$5.5 Billion**

Market Capitalization: **$8.35 Billion (Mid-Cap)**

Common Shares Outstanding: **238 Million**

Earnings per Share: **$2.18**

Annual Dividend: **$1.00**

Paying Dividends Since: **2010**

Direct Stock Purchase Plan Summary

Transfer Agent: **Computershare**
Transfer Agent website: www-us.computershare.com
Phone: 1-877-745-9312

New Account Investment Options:
One-time minimum purchase by either a check or an authorized one-time deduction from a savings or checking account: **$250.00** or the **$250.00** is waived for a minimum on-going investment of **$25.00** for 5 consecutive months.

Existing Shareholders:
Minimum share required to enroll for existing shareholders: **1**
Optional Cash Purchase Minimum: **$50.00**
Optional Cash Purchase Frequency: **Weekly**
Maximum One Time Investment: **$100,000.00 per year**
Stock Certificate issued upon request: **Yes**
Dividend Frequency: **Quarterly**

Plan Fees:
Initial Set up Fee: **$15.00**
Cash Purchase Fee: **$0.00**
On-going Automatic Investment Fee: **$0.00**
Cash Purchase Processing Fee (per share): **$0.00**
Dividend Reinvestment Fee: **$0.00**
Batch Order Sale Fee: **$15.00**
Market Order Sale Fee: **$25.00**
Batch and Market Order Processing Fee: **$0.12 per share**

How much stock does the first $50 buy? :
Initial Investment: **$50.00**
  Minus Initial Set up Fee: **$15.00**
  Cash Purchase Fee: **$0.00**
  Cash Purchase Processing Fee: **$0.00**
Total Investment: **$35.00**, Sample Stock Price: **$35.89**
Total Shares Purchased: $35.00/$35.89 = **.975202**

Entertainment Properties   19

30 West Pershing Road
Kansas City, Missouri 641080
(816) 472-1700
Company website: **www.eprkc.com**

Company Description

Entertainment Properties Trust, is a self-administered real estate investment trust (REIT). EPR develops, owns, leases and finances properties for consumer preferred businesses. As of December 31, 2009, the Company's real estate portfolio consisted of 95 mega-plex theatre properties (including four joint venture properties) located in 33 states, the District of Columbia and Ontario, Canada; nine theatre anchored entertainment retail centers (including three joint venture properties) located in four states and Ontario, Canada, and land parcels leased to restaurant and retail operators or available for development adjacent to several of its theatre properties.

Basic Company Statistics

New York Stock Exchange: **EPR**

Industry: **REIT-Retail**

Index Membership: **S&P 600**

Annual Revenue: **$270 Million**

Market Capitalization: **$2.1 Billion (Small-Cap)**

Common Shares Outstanding: **46 Million**

Earnings per Share: **$3.15**

Annual Dividend: **$2.60**

Paying Dividends Since: **1998**

Direct Stock Purchase Plan Summary

Transfer Agent: **Computershare**
Transfer Agent website: www-us.computershare.com
Phone: 1-781-575-2879

New Account Investment Options:
One-time minimum purchase by either a check or an authorized one-time deduction from a savings or checking account: **$200.00** or the **$200.00** is waived for a minimum on-going investment of **$50.00** for 4 consecutive months.

Existing Shareholders:
Minimum share required to enroll for existing shareholders: **1**
Optional Cash Purchase Minimum: **$50.00**
Optional Cash Purchase Frequency: **Weekly**
Maximum One Time Investment: **$120,000.00 per year**
Stock Certificate issued upon request: **Yes**
Dividend Frequency: **Quarterly**

Plan Fees:
Initial Set up Fee: **$0.00**
Cash Purchase Fee: **$0.00**
On-going Automatic Investment Fee: **$0.00**
Cash Purchase Processing Fee (per share): **$0.00**
Dividend Reinvestment Fee: **$0.00**
Batch Order Sale Fee: **$10.00**
Market Order Sale Fee: **$20.00**
Batch and Market Order Processing Fee: **$0.12 per share**

How much stock does the first $50 buy? :
Initial Investment: **$50.00**
  Minus Initial Set up Fee: **$0.00**
  Cash Purchase Fee: **$0.00**
  Cash Purchase Processing Fee: **$0.00**
Total Investment: **$50.00**, Sample Stock Price: **$47.31**
Total Shares Purchased: $50.00/$47.31 = **1.056859**

Exxon Mobil Corporation 20

5959 Las Colinas Boulevard
Irving, TX 75039
(972) 444-1000
Company website: www.exxonmobil.com

Company Description

Exxon Mobil Corporation (Exxon Mobil) is a manufacturer and marketer of commodity petrochemicals, including olefins, aromatics, polyethylene and polypropylene plastics and a range of specialty products. It also has interests in electric power generation facilities. The company has several divisions and hundreds of affiliates with names that include ExxonMobil, Exxon, Esso or Mobil. Divisions and affiliated companies of ExxonMobil operate or market products in the United States and other countries of the world. Their principal business is energy, involving exploration for, and production of, crude oil and natural gas, manufacture of petroleum products and transportation and sale of crude oil, natural gas and petroleum products.

Basic Company Statistics

New York Stock Exchange: **XOM**

Industry: **Oil & Gas**

Index Memberships: **Dow 30, S&P 500**

Annual Revenue: **$310 Billion**

Market Capitalization: **$290.76 Billion (Large-Cap)**

Common Shares Outstanding: **5.09 Billion**

Earnings per Share: **$3.98**

Annual Dividend: **$1.76**

Paying Dividends Since: **1882**

Direct Stock Purchase Plan Summary

Transfer Agent: **Computershare**
Transfer Agent website: www-us.computershare.com
Phone: 1-800-252-1800

New Account Investment Options:
One-time minimum purchase by either a check or an authorized one-time deduction from a savings or checking account: **$250.00** or the **$250.00** is waived for a minimum on-going investment of **$50.00** for 5 consecutive months.

Existing Shareholders:
Minimum share required to enroll for existing shareholders: **1**
Optional Cash Purchase Minimum: **$50.00**
Optional Cash Purchase Frequency: **Weekly**
Maximum One Time Investment: **$250,000.00 per year**
Stock Certificate issued upon request: **Yes**
Dividend Frequency: **Quarterly**

Plan Fees:
Initial Set up Fee: **$0.00**
Cash Purchase Fee: **$0.00**
On-going Automatic Investment Fee: **$0.00**
Cash Purchase Processing Fee (per share): **$0.00**
Dividend Reinvestment Fee: **$0.00**
Batch Order Sale Fee: **$15.00**
Market Order Sale Fee: **$25.00**
Batch and Market Order Processing Fee: **$0.12 per share**

How much stock does the first $50 buy? :
Initial Investment: **$50.00**
  Minus Initial Set up Fee: **$0.00**
  Cash Purchase Fee: **$0.00**
  Cash Purchase Processing Fee: **$0.00**
Total Investment: **$50.00**, Sample Stock Price: **$66.34**
Total Shares Purchased: $50.00/$66.34 = **.753693**

Frontier Communications Corporation — 21

3 High Ridge Park
Stamford, Connecticut 06905
(203) 614-5044
Company website: **www.frontier.com**

Company Description

Frontier Communications Corporation (Frontier), formerly Citizens Communications Company, is a communications company providing services to rural areas and small and medium-sized towns and cities. It provides communications services to residential and business customers in its markets. It offers a variety of voice, data, Internet, and television services that are available as bundled or packaged solutions and for some products, a la carte. Its services include access services; local services; long distance services; data and Internet services; directory services; television services, and wireless services.

Basic Company Statistics

New York Stock Exchange: **FTR**

Industry: **Telecommunication Services**

Index Membership: **S&P 500**

Annual Revenue: **$2.1 Billion**

Market Capitalization: **$8.4 Billion (Mid-Cap)**

Common Shares Outstanding: **312 Million**

Earnings per Share: **$0.42**

Annual Dividend: **$0.75**

Paying Dividends Since: **2004**

Direct Stock Purchase Plan Summary

Transfer Agent: **Computershare**
Transfer Agent website: www-us.computershare.com
Phone: 1-781-575-2879

New Account Investment Options:
One-time minimum purchase by either a check or an authorized one-time deduction from a savings or checking account: **$250.00** or the **$250.00** is waived for a minimum on-going investment of **$50.00** for 5 consecutive months.

Existing Shareholders:
Minimum share required to enroll for existing shareholders: **1**
Optional Cash Purchase Minimum: **$50.00**
Optional Cash Purchase Frequency: **Weekly**
Maximum One Time Investment: **$250,000.00 per year**
Stock Certificate issued upon request: **Yes**
Dividend Frequency: **Quarterly**

Plan Fees:
Initial Set up Fee: **$10.00**
Cash Purchase Fee: **$5.00**
On-going Automatic Investment Fee: **$2.50**
Cash Purchase Processing Fee (per share): **$0.05**
Dividend Reinvestment Fee: **5% of up to a maximum of $3.00**
Batch Order Sale Fee: **$15.00**
Market Order Sale Fee: **$25.00**
Batch and Market Order Processing Fee: **$0.12 per share**

How much stock does the first $50 buy? :
Initial Investment: **$50.00**
  Minus Initial Set up Fee: **$10.00**
  Cash Purchase Fee: **$5.00**
  Cash Purchase Processing Fee: **$0.05**
Total Investment: **$34.95**, Sample Stock Price: **$8.79**
Total Shares Purchased: $34.95/$8.79 = **3.976109**

Glimcher Realty Trust 22

180 East Broad Street
Columbus, Ohio 43215
(614) 621-9000
Company website: **www.glimcher.com**

Company Description

Glimcher Realty Trust is an integrated real estate investment trust (REIT). The Company owns leases, acquires, develops and operates a portfolio of retail properties consisting of enclosed and regional malls (Malls) and community shopping centers (Community Centers). As of December 31, 2009, the Malls and Community Centers (the Properties) consisted of 21 Malls (two of which are partially owned through joint ventures) containing an aggregate of 19.9 million square feet of gross lease able area and four Community Centers containing an aggregate of 769,000 square feet square feet of GLA.

Basic Company Statistics

New York Stock Exchange: **GRT**

Industry: **REIT - Retail**

Index Membership: **None**

Annual Revenue: **$308 Million**

Market Capitalization: **$458 Million (Small-Cap)**

Common Shares Outstanding: **68.9 Million**

Earnings per Share: **$1.50**

Annual Dividend: **$.40**

Paying Dividends Since: **1994**

Direct Stock Purchase Plan Summary

Transfer Agent: **Computershare**
Transfer Agent website: www-us.computershare.com
Phone: 1-800-738-4931

New Account Investment Options:
One-time minimum purchase by either a check or an authorized one-time deduction from a savings or checking account: **$50.00**

Existing Shareholders:
Minimum share required to enroll for existing shareholders: **1**
Optional Cash Purchase Minimum: **$50.00**
Optional Cash Purchase Frequency: **Weekly**
Maximum One Time Investment: **$12,000.00 per year**
Stock Certificate issued upon request: **Yes**
Dividend Frequency: **Quarterly**

Plan Fees:
Initial Set up Fee: **$0.00**
Cash Purchase Fee: **$0.00**
On-going Automatic Investment Fee: **$2.50**
Cash Purchase Processing Fee: **$0.00 per share**
Dividend Reinvestment Fee: **$0.00**
Batch Order Sale Fee: **$15.00**
Batch Order Processing Fee: **$0.10 per share**

> **How much stock does the first $50 buy? :**
> Initial Investment: **$50.00**
>   Minus Initial Set up Fee: **$0.00**
>   Cash Purchase Fee: **$0.00**
>   Cash Purchase Processing Fee: **$0.00**
> Total Investment: **$50.00**, Sample Stock Price: **$7.51**
> **Total Shares Purchased:** $50.00/$7.51 = **6.65779**

Hersey Company (The)   23

100 Crystal A Drive
Hershey, Pennsylvania 17033
(717) 534-4200
Company website: **www.herseys.com**

Company Description

The Hershey Company is a manufacturer of chocolate and sugar confectionery products. The Company's principal product groups include chocolate and confectionery products; snack products; gum and mint refreshment products; and pantry items, such as baking ingredients, toppings and beverages. The Company manufactures, markets, sells and distributes various package types of chocolate and confectionery products, pantry items, and gum and mint refreshment products under more than 80 brand names.

Basic Company Statistics

New York Stock Exchange: **HSY**

Industry: **Package Foods**

Index Membership: **S&P 500**

Annual Revenue: **$5.2 Billion**

Market Capitalization: **$8.3 Billion (Mid-Cap)**

Common Shares Outstanding: **227 Million**

Earnings per Share: **$1.90**

Annual Dividend: **$1.28**

Paying Dividends Since: **1930**

Direct Stock Purchase Plan Summary

Transfer Agent: **Bank of New York Mellon**
Transfer Agent website: www.melloninvestor.com
Phone: 1-800-851-4216

New Account Investment Options:
One-time minimum purchase by either a check or an authorized one-time deduction from a savings or checking account: **$250.00** or the **$250.00** is waived for a minimum on-going investment of **$25.00** for 10 consecutive months.

Existing Shareholders:
Minimum share required to enroll for existing shareholders: **1**
Optional Cash Purchase Minimum: **$25.00**
Optional Cash Purchase Frequency: **Weekly**
Maximum One Time Investment: **$10,000.00**
Stock Certificate issued upon request: **Yes**
Dividend Frequency: **Quarterly**

Plan Fees:
Initial Set up Fee: **$15.00**
Cash Purchase Fee via check: **$5.00**
Cash Purchase Fee via automatic debit: **$2.00**
Cash Purchase Processing Fee (per share): **$0.06**
Dividend Reinvestment Fee: **$0.00**
Market Order Sale Fee: **$15.00**
Market Order Processing Fee: **$0.12 per share**

How much stock does the first $50 buy? :
Initial Investment: **$50.00**
  Minus Initial Set up Fee: **$15.00**
  Cash Purchase Fee via automatic debit: **$2.00**
  Cash Purchase Processing Fee (per share): **$0.03**
Total Investment: **$32.97**, Sample Stock Price: **$49.91**
Total Shares Purchased: $32.97/$49.91 = **.6606**

Home Depot, Inc. (The)   24

2455 Paces Ferry Road, NW
Atlanta, Georgia 30339
(770) 433-8211
Company website: **www.homedepot.com**

Company Description

The Home Depot, Inc. is a home improvement retailer. The Home Depot stores sell an assortment of building materials, home improvement and lawn and garden products and provide a number of services. Home Depot stores average approximately 105,000 square feet of enclosed space, with approximately 24,000 additional square feet of outside garden area. As of January 31, 2010, it had 2,244 Home Depot stores located throughout the United States, including the Commonwealth of Puerto Rico and the territories of the United States Virgin Islands and Guam (U.S.), Canada, China and Mexico.

Basic Company Statistics

New York Stock Exchange: **HD**

Industry: **Retail**

Index Memberships: **Dow 30, S&P 500**

Annual Revenue: **$66.17 Billion**

Market Capitalization: **$54.98 Billion (Large-Cap)**

Common Shares Outstanding: **1.66 Billion**

Earnings per Share: **$1.55**

Annual Dividend: **$0.95**

Paying Dividends Since: **1987**

Direct Stock Purchase Plan Summary

Transfer Agent: **Computershare**
Transfer Agent website: www-us.computershare.com
Phone: 1-800-577-0177

New Account Investment Options:
One-time minimum purchase by either a check or an authorized one-time deduction from a savings or checking account: **$500.00** or the **$500.00** is waived for a minimum on-going investment of **$50.00** for 10 consecutive months.

Existing Shareholders:
Minimum share required to enroll for existing shareholders: **1**
Optional Cash Purchase Minimum: **$50.00**
Optional Cash Purchase Frequency: **Weekly**
Maximum One Time Investment: **$250,000.00 per year**
Stock Certificate issued upon request: **Yes**
Dividend Frequency: **Quarterly**

Plan Fees:
Initial Set up Fee: **$5.00**
Cash Purchase Fee: **$2.50**
On-going Automatic Investment Fee: **$2.50**
Cash Purchase Processing Fee (per share): **$0.05**
Dividend Reinvestment Fee: **5% up to a maximum of $2.50**
Batch Order Sale Fee: **$15.00**
Market Order Sale Fee: **$25.00**
Batch and Market Order Processing Fee: **$0.15 per share**

How much stock does the first $50 buy? :
Initial Investment: **$50.00**
  Minus Initial set up: **$5.00**
  Cash Purchase Fee: **$2.50**
  Cash Purchase Processing Fee (per share): **$0.05**
Total Investment: **$42.45**, Sample Stock Price: **$31.48**
Total Shares Purchased: $42.45/$31.48 = **1.34847**

IBM Corporation   25

1 New Orchard Road
Armonk, New York 10504
(914) 499-1900
Company website: **www.ibm.com**

Company Description

International Business Machines Corporation (IBM) is an information technology company. The company operates under five segments: Global Technology Services segment (GTS); Global Business Services segment (GBS); Software segment; System and Technology segment, and Global Financing segment. In October 2009, IBM Corporation completed its acquisition of SPSS Inc. In November 2009, IBM acquired Guardium. In January 2010, IBM announced the completion of its acquisition of Lombardi. In February 2010, the Company acquired Intelliden Inc. In March 2010, the company completed the acquisition of National Interest Security Company, LLC. In April 2010, the company acquired Cast Iron.

Basic Company Statistics

New York Stock Exchange: **IBM**

Industry: **Information Technology**

Index Memberships: **Dow 30, S&P 500**

Annual Revenue: **$95.7 Billion**

Market Capitalization: **$177.91 Billion (Large-Cap)**

Common Shares Outstanding: **1.26 Billion**

Earnings per Share: **$10.01**

Annual Dividend: **$2.60**

Paying Dividends Since: **1916**

Direct Stock Purchase Plan Summary

Transfer Agent: **Computershare**
Transfer Agent website: www-us.computershare.com
Phone: 1-888-426-6700

New Account Investment Options:
One-time minimum purchase by either a check or an authorized one-time deduction from a savings or checking account: **$500.00** or the **$500.00** is waived for a minimum on-going investment of **$50.00** for 10 consecutive months.

Existing Shareholders:
Minimum share required to enroll for existing shareholders: **1**
Optional Cash Purchase Minimum: **$50.00**
Optional Cash Purchase Frequency: **Weekly**
Maximum One Time Investment: **$250,000.00 per year**
Stock Certificate issued upon request: **Yes**
Dividend Frequency: **Quarterly**

Plan Fees:
Initial Set up Fee: **$15.00**
Cash Purchase Fee: **$5.00**
On-going Automatic Investment Fee: **$1.00**
Cash Purchase Processing Fee (per share): **$0.00**
Dividend Reinvestment Fee: **2% up to a maximum of $3.00**
Batch Order Sale Fee: **$15.00**
Market Order Sale Fee: **$25.00**
Batch and Market Order Processing Fee: **$0.10 per share**

How much stock does the first $50 buy? :
Initial Investment: **$50.00**
  Minus Initial Set up Fee: **$15.00**
  Cash Purchase Fee: **$5.00**
  Cash Purchase Processing Fee (per share): **$0.00**
Total Investment: **$35.00**, Sample Stock Price: **$139.67**
Total Shares Purchased: $35.00/$139.67 = **.250591**

Intel Corporation 26

2200 Mission College Boulevard
Santa Clara, California 95054
(408) 765-8080
Company website: **www.intel.com**

Company Description

Intel Corporation is a semiconductor chip maker, developing advanced integrated digital technology products, primarily integrated circuits, for industries, such as computing and communications. The Company designs and manufactures computing and communications components, such as microprocessors, chipsets, motherboards, and wireless and wired connectivity products, as well as platforms that incorporate these components. It operates in nine operating segments: PC Client Group, Data Center Group, Embedded and Communications Group, Digital Home Group, Ultra-Mobility Group, NAND Solutions Group, Wind River Software Group, Software and Services Group and Digital Health Group. During the fiscal year ended December 26, 2009 it acquired Wind River Systems, Inc.

Basic Company Statistics

NASDAQ: **INTC**

Industry: **Information Technology**

Index Memberships: **Dow 30, S&P 500, NASDAQ 100**

Annual Revenue: **$35.1 Billion**

Market Capitalization: **$104.57 Billion (Large-Cap)**

Common Shares Outstanding: **5.56 Billion**

Earnings per Share: **$0.77**

Annual Dividend: **$0.63**

Paying Dividends Since: **1992**

Direct Stock Purchase Plan Summary

Transfer Agent: **Computershare**
Transfer Agent website: www-us.computershare.com
Phone: 1-800-298-0146

New Account Investment Options:
One-time minimum purchase by either a check or an authorized one-time deduction from a savings or checking account: **$250.00** or the **$250.00** is waived for a minimum on-going investment of **$50.00** for 5 consecutive months.

Existing Shareholders:
Minimum share required to enroll for existing shareholders: **1**
Optional Cash Purchase Minimum: **$50.00**
Optional Cash Purchase Frequency: **Weekly**
Maximum One Time Investment: **$100,000.00 per year**
Stock Certificate issued upon request: **Yes**
Dividend Frequency: **Quarterly**

Plan Fees:
Initial Set up Fee: **$10.00**
Cash Purchase Fee: **$5.00**
On-going Automatic Investment Fee: **$2.50**
Cash Purchase Processing Fee (per share): **$0.10**
Dividend Reinvestment Fee: **5% up to a maximum of $3.00**
Batch Order Sale Fee: **$15.00**
Market Order Sale Fee: **$25.00**
Batch and Market Order Processing Fee: **$0.10 per share**

How much stock does the first $50 buy? :
Initial Investment: **$50.00**
  Minus Initial set up: **$10.00**
  Cash Purchase Fee: **$5.00**
  Cash Purchase Processing Fee (per share): **$0.10**
Total Investment: **$34.90**, Sample Stock Price: **$19.83**
Total Shares Purchased: $34.90/$19.83 = **1.759960**

J.C. Penney Company, Inc.   27

6501 Legacy Drive
Plano, Texas 75024
(972) 431-1000
Company website: **www.jcpenney.net**

Company Description

J. C. Penney Company, Inc. is a holding company whose principal operating subsidiary is J. C. Penney Corporation, Inc. The company is a retailer, operating 1,108 J.C. Penney department stores in 49 states and Puerto Rico as of January 30, 2010. Its business consists of selling merchandise and services to consumers through its department stores and Direct (Internet/catalog) channels. JC Penney sells family apparel and footwear, accessories, fine and fashion jewelry, beauty products through Sephora inside J. C. Penney and home furnishings.

Basic Company Statistics

New York Stock Exchange: **JCP**

Industry: **Retail**

Index Membership: **S&P 500**

Annual Revenue: **$17.55 Billion**

Market Capitalization: **$8 Billion (Large-Cap)**

Common Shares Outstanding: **236.4 Million**

Earnings per Share: **$2.54**

Annual Dividend: **$0.80**

Paying Dividends Since: **1922**

Direct Stock Purchase Plan Summary

Transfer Agent: **Bank of New York Mellon**
Transfer Agent website: www.melloninvestor.com
Phone: 1-800-842-9470

New Account Investment Options:
One-time minimum purchase by either a check or an authorized one-time deduction from a savings or checking account: **$250.00** or the **$250.00** is waived with a minimum on-going investment of **$25.00** for 10 consecutive months.

Existing Shareholders:
Minimum share required to enroll for existing shareholders: **1**
Optional Cash Purchase Minimum: **$25.00**
Optional Cash Purchase Frequency: **Weekly**
Maximum One Time Investment: **$10,000.00**
Stock Certificate issued upon request: **Yes**
Dividend Frequency: **Quarterly**

Plan Fees:
Initial Set up Fee: **$10.00**
Cash Purchase Fee via check: **$1.50**
Cash Purchase Fee via automatic debit: **$1.50**
Cash Purchase Processing Fee (per share): **$0.06**
Dividend Reinvestment Fee: **$0.00**
Market Order Sale Fee: **$15.00**
Market Order Processing Fee: **$0.06 per share**

How much stock does the first $50 buy? :
Initial Investment: **$50.00**
  Minus Initial Set up Fee: **$10.00**
  Cash Purchase Fee via automatic debit: **$1.50**
  Cash Purchase Processing Fee (per share): **$0.03**
Total Investment: **$38.47**, Sample Stock Price: **$32.55**
Total Shares Purchased: $38.47/$32.55 = **1.181874**

J.M. Smuckers Company (The)   28

1 Strawberry Lane
Orrville, Ohio 44667
(330) 682-3000
Company website: **www.smuckers.com**

Company Description

The J. M. Smucker Company is in the manufacturing and marketing of branded food products business. The majority of the company's sales are in the United States. The Company's operations outside the United States are principally in Canada although products are exported to other countries, as well. Sales outside the United States represented approximately 10 % of total consolidated company sales during the fiscal year ends April 30, 2010. The Company's branded food products include a portfolio of brands that are sold to consumers through retail outlets in North America.

Basic Company Statistics

New York Stock Exchange: **SJM**

Industry: **Processed & Packaged Goods**

Index Memberships: **S&P 500**

Annual Revenue: **$3.75 Billion**

Market Capitalization: **$7.5 Billion (Large-Cap)**

Common Shares Outstanding: **119.5 Million**

Earnings per Share: **$3.12**

Annual Dividend: **$1.60**

Paying Dividends Since: **1949**

Direct Stock Purchase Plan Summary

Transfer Agent: **Computershare**
Transfer Agent website: www-us.computershare.com
Phone: 1-800-456-1169

New Account Investment Options:
One-time minimum purchase by either a check or an authorized one-time deduction from a savings or checking account: **$250.00** or the **$250.00** is waived with a minimum on-going investment of **$25.00** for 10 consecutive months.

Existing Shareholders:
Minimum share required to enroll for existing shareholders: **1**
Optional Cash Purchase Minimum: **$25.00**
Optional Cash Purchase Frequency: **Weekly**
Maximum One Time Investment: **$50,000.00 per year**
Stock Certificate issued upon request: **Yes**
Dividend Frequency: **Quarterly**

Plan Fees:
Initial Set up Fee: **$10.00**
Cash Purchase Fee: **$5.00**
On-going Automatic Investment Fee: **$1.50**
Cash Purchase Processing Fee (per share): **$0.10**
Dividend Reinvestment Fee: **$0.00**
Batch Sale Fee: **$10.00**
Market Order Sale Fee: **$25.00**
Batch and Market Order Processing Fee: **$0.10 per share**

How much stock does the first $50 buy? :
Initial Investment: **$50.00**
  Minus Initial Set up Fee: **$10.00**
  Cash Purchase Fee: **$5.00**
  Cash Purchase Processing Fee (per share): **$.10**
Total Investment: **$34.90**, Sample Stock Price: **$63.00**
Total Shares Purchased: $34.90/$63.00 = **.553968**

JPMorgan Chase & Company   29

270 Park Avenue
New York, New York 10017
(212) 270-6000
Company website: **www.jpmorganchase.com**

Company Description

JPMorgan Chase & Co. is a financial holding company. JPMorgan Chase's principal bank subsidiaries are JPMorgan Chase Bank, National Association (JPMorgan Chase Bank, N.A.), a national banking association with United States branches in 23 states, and Chase Bank USA, National Association (Chase Bank USA, N.A.), a national banking association that is the Firm's credit card–issuing bank. JPMorgan Chase's principal nonbank subsidiary is J.P. Morgan Securities Inc. (JPMorgan Securities), its United States investment banking firm. Its activities are organized into six business segments: Investment Bank, Retail Financial Services (RFS), Card Services (CS), Commercial Banking (CB), Treasury & Securities Services (TSS) and Asset Management (AM). Its wholesale businesses comprise the Investment Bank,

Basic Company Statistics

New York Stock Exchange: **JPM**

Industry: **Banking**

Index Memberships: **Dow 30, S&P 500**

Annual Revenue: **$115.6 Billion**

Market Capitalization: **$147.3 Billion (Large-Cap)**

Common Shares Outstanding: **3.96 Billion**

Earnings per Share: **$2.24**

Annual Dividend: **$0.20**

Paying Dividends Since: **1827**

Direct Stock Purchase Plan Summary

Transfer Agent: **Bank of New York Mellon**
Transfer Agent website: www.melloninvestor.com
Phone: 1-800-758-4651

New Account Investment Options:
One-time minimum purchase by either a check or an authorized one-time deduction from a savings or checking account: **$250.00** or the **$250.00** is waived with a minimum on-going investment of **$50.00** for 5 consecutive months.

Existing Shareholders:
Minimum share required to enroll for existing shareholders: **1**
Optional Cash Purchase Minimum: **$50.00**
Optional Cash Purchase Frequency: **Weekly**
Maximum One Time Investment: **$250,000.00 per year**
Stock Certificate issued upon request: **Yes**
Dividend Frequency: **Quarterly**

Plan Fees:
Initial Set up Fee: **$15.00**
Cash Purchase Fee via check: **$5.00**
Cash Purchase Fee via automatic debit: **$2.00**
Cash Purchase Processing Fee (per share): **$0.03**
Dividend Reinvestment Fee: **$0.00**
Market Order Sale Fee: **$15.00**
Market Order Processing Fee: **$0.05 per share**

How much stock does the first $50 buy? :
Initial Investment: **$50.00**
  Minus Initial Set up Fee: **$15.00**
  Cash Purchase Fee via automatic debit: **$2.00**
  Cash Purchase Processing Fee (per share): **$0.03**
Total Investment: **$32.97**, Sample Stock Price: **$38.09**
Total Shares Purchased: $32.97/$38.09 = **.8656**

Kimberly-Clark Corp. 30

P.O. Box 619100
Dallas, Texas 75261
(972) 281-1200
Company website: **www.kimberly-clark.com**

Company Description

Kimberly-Clark Corporation is a global health and hygiene company focused on product innovation and building its personal care, consumer tissue, K-C Professional and Other and health care brands. The Company is principally engaged in the manufacturing and marketing of a range of health and hygiene products worldwide. The Company operates in four segments: Personal Care; Consumer Tissue; K-C Professional & Other, and Health Care. The Personal Care segment manufactures and markets disposable diapers, training and youth pants, and swim pants; baby wipes; feminine and incontinence care products, and related products. The Consumer Tissue segment manufactures and markets facial and bathroom tissue and paper towels.

Basic Company Statistics

New York Stock Exchange: **KMB**

Industry: **Personal Products**

Index Membership: **S&P 500**

Annual Revenue: **$19.1 Billion**

Market Capitalization: **$26.61 Billion (Large-Cap)**

Common Shares Outstanding: **409.3 Million**

Earnings per Share: **$4.52**

Annual Dividend: **$2.64**

Paying Dividends Since: **1935**

Direct Stock Purchase Plan Summary

Transfer Agent: **Computershare**
Transfer Agent website: www-us.computershare.com
Phone: 1-800-730-4001

New Account Investment Options:
One-time minimum purchase by either a check or an authorized one-time deduction from a savings or checking account: **$250.00** or the **$250.00** is waived with a minimum on-going investment of **$50.00** for 5 consecutive months.

Existing Shareholders:
Minimum share required to enroll for existing shareholders: **1**
Optional Cash Purchase Minimum: **$50.00**
Optional Cash Purchase Frequency: **Weekly**
Maximum One Time Investment: **$100,000.00 per year**
Stock Certificate issued upon request: **Yes**
Dividend Frequency: **Quarterly**

Plan Fees:
Initial Set up Fee: **$10.00**
Cash Purchase Fee: **$5.00**
On-going Automatic Investment Fee: **$2.50**
Cash Purchase Processing Fee (per share): **$0.05**
Dividend Reinvestment Fee: **$0.00**
Batch Order Sale Fee: **$15.00**
Market Order Sale Fee: **$25.00**
Batch and Market Order Processing Fee: **$0.15 per share**

How much stock does the first $50 buy? :
Initial Investment: **$50.00**
  Minus Initial Set up Fee: **$10.00**
  Cash Purchase Fee: **$5.00**
  Cash Purchase Processing Fee (per share): **$0.05**
Total Investment: **$34.95**, Sample Stock Price: **$66.56**
Total Shares Purchased: $34.95/$66.56 = **.272248**

Lockheed Martin Corporation   31

6801 Rockledge Drive
Bethesda, Maryland 20817
(301) 897-6000
Company website: **www.lockheedmartin.com**

Company Description

Lockheed Martin Corporation is a global security company engaged in the research, design, development, manufacture, integration of advanced technology systems and products. It also provides a range of management, engineering, technical, scientific, logistic, and information services. The Company operates in four business segments: Aeronautics, Electronic Systems, Information Systems & Global Services, and Space Systems. In September 2008, Lockheed Martin Corporation acquired Aculight Corporation. In January 2009, it completed its acquisition of Universal Systems & Technology, Inc.

Basic Company Statistics

New York Stock Exchange: **LMT**

Industry: **Defense Products & Services**

Index Membership: **S&P 500**

Annual Revenue: **$45.1 Billion**

Market Capitalization: **$75.1 Billion (Large-Cap)**

Common Shares Outstanding: **362.5 Million**

Earnings per Share: **$7.78**

Annual Dividend: **$3.00**

Paying Dividends Since: **1995**

Direct Stock Purchase Plan Summary

Transfer Agent: **Computershare**
Transfer Agent website: www-us.computershare.com
Phone: 1-877-498-8861

New Account Investment Options:
One-time minimum purchase by either a check or an authorized one-time deduction from a savings or checking account: **$250.00** or the **$250.00** is waived with a minimum on-going investment of **$50.00** for 5 consecutive months.

Existing Shareholders:
Minimum share required to enroll for existing shareholders: **1**
Optional Cash Purchase Minimum: **$50.00**
Optional Cash Purchase Frequency: **Weekly**
Maximum One Time Investment: **$50,000,000.00 per year**
Stock Certificate issued upon request: **Yes**
Dividend Frequency: **Quarterly**

Plan Fees:
Initial Set up Fee: **$0.00**
Cash Purchase Fee: **$0.00**
On-going Automatic Investment Fee: **$0.00**
Cash Purchase Processing Fee (per share): **$0.00**
Dividend Reinvestment Fee: **$3.00**
Batch Order Sale Fee: **$15.00**
Market Order Sale Fee: **$25.00**
Batch and Market Order Processing Fee: **$0.12 per share**

How much stock does the first $50 buy? :
Initial Investment: **$50.00**
  Minus Initial Set up Fee: **$0.00**
  Cash Purchase Fee: **$0.00**
  Cash Purchase Processing Fee (per share): **$0.00**
Total Investment: **$50.00**, Sample Stock Price: **$69.16**
Total Shares Purchased: $50.00/$69.16 = **.722961**

Lowes Companies 32

1000 Lowes Boulevard
Mooresville, North Carolina 28117
(704) 758-1000
Company website: **www.lowes.com**

Company Description

Lowe's Companies, Inc. (Lowe's) is a home improvement retailer. As of January 29, 2010, the Company operated 1,710 stores, consisted of 1,694 stores across 50 United States and 16 stores in Canada. Its 1,710 stores represent approximately 193 million square feet of retail selling space. The Company serves homeowners, renters and commercial business customers. Homeowners and renters primarily consist of do-it-yourself (DIY) customers and do-it-for-me (DIFM) customers who utilize its installed sales programs, as well as others buying for personal and family use.

Basic Company Statistics

New York Stock Exchange: **LOW**

Industry: **Retail**

Index Membership: **S&P 500**

Annual Revenue: **$48.2 Billion**

Market Capitalization: **$30.8 Billion (Large-Cap)**

Common Shares Outstanding: **1.4 Billion**

Earnings per Share: **$1.21**

Annual Dividend: **$0.44**

Paying Dividends Since: **1961**

Direct Stock Purchase Plan Summary

Transfer Agent: **Computershare**
Transfer Agent website: www-us.computershare.com
Phone: 1-877-282-1174

New Account Investment Options:
One-time minimum purchase by either a check or an authorized one-time deduction from a savings or checking account: **$250.00** or the **$250.00** is waived with a minimum on-going investment of **$50.00** for 5 consecutive months.

Existing Shareholders:
Minimum share required to enroll for existing shareholders: **1**
Optional Cash Purchase Minimum: **$50.00**
Optional Cash Purchase Frequency: **Weekly**
Maximum One Time Investment: **$250,000.00 per year**
Stock Certificate issued upon request: **Yes**
Dividend Frequency: **Quarterly**

Plan Fees:
Initial Set up Fee: **$5.00**
Cash Purchase Fee: **$2.50**
On-going Automatic Investment Fee: **$2.50**
Cash Purchase Processing Fee (per share): **$0.05**
Dividend Reinvestment Fee: **$0.00**
Batch Sale Fee: **$10.00**
Market Order Sale Fee: **$25.00**
Batch and Market Order Processing Fee: **$0.12 per share**

How much stock does the first $50 buy? :
Initial Investment: **$50.00**
  Minus Initial Set up Fee: **$5.00**
  Cash Purchase Fee: **$2.50**
  Cash Purchase Processing Fee (per share): **$0.05**
Total Investment: **$42.45**, Sample Stock Price: **$22.66**
Total Shares Purchased: $42.45/$22.66 = **1.873345**

Macerich Company (The) — 33

401 Wilshire Boulevard
Suite 700
Santa Monica, California 90401
(310) 394-6000
Company website: **www.macerich.com**

Company Description

The Macerich Company is involved in the acquisition, ownership, development, redevelopment, management and leasing of regional and community shopping centers located throughout the United States. The Company is the sole general partner of, and owns a majority of the ownership interests in, The Macerich Partnership, L.P (the Operating Partnership). As of December 31, 2009, the Operating Partnership owned or had an ownership interest in 72 regional shopping centers and 14 community shopping centers.

Basic Company Statistics

New York Stock Exchange: **MAC**

Industry: **REIT - Retail**

Index Membership: **S&P 1500**

Annual Revenue: **$805.7 Million**

Market Capitalization: **$5.5 Billion (Mid-Cap)**

Common Shares Outstanding: **130.1 Million**

Earnings per Share: **$3.70**

Annual Dividend: **$2.00**

Paying Dividends Since: **1994**

Direct Stock Purchase Plan Summary

Transfer Agent: **Computershare**
Transfer Agent website: **www-us.computershare.com**
Phone: 1-781-575-2726

New Account Investment Options:
One-time minimum purchase by either a check or an authorized one-time deduction from a savings or checking account: **$250.00** or the **$250.00** is waived with a minimum on-going investment of **$50.00** for 5 consecutive months.

Existing Shareholders:
Minimum share required to enroll for existing shareholders: **1**
Optional Cash Purchase Minimum: **$50.00**
Optional Cash Purchase Frequency: **Weekly**
Maximum One Time Investment: **$250,000.00 per year**
Stock Certificate issued upon request: **Yes**
Dividend Frequency: **Quarterly**

Plan Fees:
Initial Set up Fee: **$0.00**
Cash Purchase Fee: **$0.00**
On-going Automatic Investment Fee: **$0.00**
Cash Purchase Processing Fee (per share): **$0.00**
Dividend Reinvestment Fee: **$0.00**
Batch Sale Fee: **$10.00**
Batch and Market Order Processing Fee: **$0.12 per share**

How much stock does the first $50 buy? :
Initial Investment: **$50.00**
 Minus Initial Set up Fee: **$0.00**
 Cash Purchase Fee: **$0.00**
 Cash Purchase Processing Fee (per share): **$0.00**
Total Investment: **$50.00**, Sample Stock Price: **$46.12**
Total Shares Purchased: $50.00/$46.12 = **1.084128**

McDonald's Corporation   34

2111 McDonald's Drive
Oak Brook, Illinois 60523
(630) 623-3000
Company website: **www.mcdonalds.com**

Company Description

McDonald's Corporation franchises and operates McDonald's restaurants in the food service industry. These restaurants serve a varied, yet limited, value-priced menu in more than 100 countries worldwide. All restaurants are operated either by the Company or by franchisees, including conventional franchisees under franchise arrangements, and foreign-affiliated markets and developmental licensees under license agreements. Independently-owned and operated distribution centers, approved by the Company, distribute products and supplies to most McDonald's restaurants. In addition, restaurant personnel are trained in the storage, handling and preparation of products and in the delivery of customer service. In February 2009, the Company sold its interest in Redbox Automated Retail, LLC.

Basic Company Statistics

New York Stock Exchange: **MCD**

Industry: **Restaurants**

Index Memberships: **Dow 30, S&P 500**

Annual Revenue: **$22.74 Billion**

Market Capitalization: **$74.63 Billion (Large-Cap)**

Common Shares Outstanding: **1.07 Billion**

Earnings per Share: **$4.11**

Annual Dividend: **$2.20**

Paying Dividends Since: **1976**

Direct Stock Purchase Plan Summary

Transfer Agent: **Computershare**
Transfer Agent website: www.us.computershare.com
Phone: 1-800-621-7825

New Account Investment Options:
One-time minimum purchase by either a check or an authorized one-time deduction from a savings or checking account: **$500.00** or the **$500.00** is waived with a minimum on-going investment of **$50.00** for 10 consecutive months.

Existing Shareholders:
Minimum shares required to enroll for existing shareholders: **10**
Optional Cash Purchase Minimum: **$50.00**
Optional Cash Purchase Frequency: **Weekly**
Maximum One Time Investment: **$250,000.00 per year**
Stock Certificate issued upon request: **Yes**
Dividend Frequency: **Quarterly**

Plan Fees:
Initial Set up Fee: **$5.00**
Cash Purchase Fee: **$6.00**
On-going Automatic Investment Fee: **$1.50**
Cash Purchase Processing Fee (per share): **$0.00**
Dividend Reinvestment Fee: **$0.00**
Batch Sale Fee: **$15.00**
Market Order Sale Fee: **$25.00**
Batch and Market Order Processing Fee: **$0.10 per share**

How much stock does the first $50 buy? :
Initial Investment: **$50.00**
  Minus Initial Set up Fee: **$5.00**
  Cash Purchase Fee: **$6.00**
  Cash Purchase Processing Fee (per share): **$0.00**
Total Investment: **.39.00**, Sample Stock Price: **$69.54**
Total Shares Purchased: $39.00/$69.54 = **.560828**

New York Community Bancorp — 35

615 Merrick Avenue
Westbury, New York 11590
(516) 683-4100
Company website: **www.mynycb.com**

Company Description

New York Community Bancorp, Inc. is a bank holding company and a producer of multi-family mortgage loans in New York City. The Company has two bank subsidiaries: New York Community Bank, has 242 branches serving customers throughout Metro New York, New Jersey, Florida, Ohio, and Arizona, and New York Commercial Bank, with 35 branches serving customers in Manhattan, Queens, Brooklyn, Long Island, and Westchester County in New York. New York Community Bank operates through seven local divisions: Queens County Savings Bank in Queens, Roslyn Savings Bank on Long Island, Richmond County Savings Bank on Staten Island, Roosevelt Savings Bank in Brooklyn, Garden State Community Bank in New Jersey, Ohio Savings Bank in Ohio, and AmTrust Bank in Florida and Arizona.

Basic Company Statistics

New York Stock Exchange: **NYB**

Industry: **Banking**

Index Membership: **S&P 1500**

Annual Revenue: **$115.6 Billion**

Market Capitalization: **$149.7 Billion (Large-Cap)**

Common Shares Outstanding: **3.98 Billion**

Earnings per Share: **$2.60**

Annual Dividend: **$.20**

Paying Dividends Since: **1827**

Direct Stock Purchase Plan Summary

Transfer Agent: **Bank of New York Mellon**
Transfer Agent website: www.melloninvestor.com
Phone: 1-866-293-6077

New Account Investment Options:
One-time minimum purchase by either a check or an authorized one-time deduction from a savings or checking account: **$50.00**

Existing Shareholders:
Minimum share required to enroll for existing shareholders: **1**
Optional Cash Purchase Minimum: **$50.00**
Optional Cash Purchase Frequency: **Weekly**
Maximum One Time Investment: **$250,000.00 per year**
Stock Certificate issued upon request: **Yes**
Dividend Frequency: **Quarterly**

Plan Fees:
Initial Set up Fee: **$15.00**
Cash Purchase Fee via check: **$5.00**
Cash Purchase Fee via automatic debit: **$2.00**
Cash Purchase Processing Fee (per share): **$0.03**
Dividend Reinvestment Fee: **$0.00**
Market Order Sale Fee: **$15.00**
Market Order Processing Fee: **$0.05 per share**

How much stock does the first $50 buy? :
Initial Investment: **$50.00**
  Minus Initial Set up Fee: **$15.00**
  Cash Purchase Fee via automatic: **$2.00**
  Cash Purchase Processing Fee (per share): **$0.03**
Total Investment: **$32.97**, Sample Stock Price: **$38.09**
Total Shares Purchased: $32.97/$38.09 = **.8656**

Newell Rubbermaid, Inc. 36

Three Glenlake Parkway
Atlanta, Georgia 30328
(770) 418-7000
Company website: **www.newellrubbermaid.com**

Company Description

Newell Rubbermaid Inc. is a global marketer of consumer and commercial products. The Company's products are marketed under a portfolio of brands, including Rubbermaid, Graco, Aprica, Levolor, Calphalon, Goody, Sharpie, Paper Mate, Dymo, Parker, Waterman, Irwin, Lenox and Technical Concepts. The Company's multi-product offering consists of consumer and commercial products in three business segments: Home & Family; Office Products; and Tools, Hardware & Commercial Products.

Basic Company Statistics

New York Stock Exchange: **NWL**

Industry: **House wares & Specialties**

Index Membership: **S&P 500**

Annual Revenue: **$5.5 Billion**

Market Capitalization: **$74.63 Billion (Mid-Cap)**

Common Shares Outstanding: **1.07 Billion**

Earnings per Share: **$4.11**

Annual Dividend: **$2.20**

Paying Dividends Since: **1976**

Direct Stock Purchase Plan Summary

Transfer Agent: **Computershare**
Transfer Agent website: www-us.computershare.com
Phone: 1-800-621-7825

New Account Investment Options:
One-time minimum purchase by either a check or an authorized one-time deduction from a savings or checking account: **$500.00** or the **$500.00** is waived with a minimum on-going investment of **$50.00** for 10 consecutive months.

Existing Shareholders:
Minimum share required to enroll for existing shareholders: **10**
Optional Cash Purchase Minimum: **$50.00**
Optional Cash Purchase Frequency: **Weekly**
Maximum One Time Investment: **$250,000.00 per year**
Stock Certificate issued upon request: **Yes**
Dividend Frequency: **Quarterly**

Plan Fees:
Initial Set up Fee: **$5.00**
Cash Purchase Fee: **$6.00**
On-going Automatic Investment Fee: **$1.50**
Cash Purchase Processing Fee (per share): **$0.00**
Dividend Reinvestment Fee: **$0.00**
Batch Sale Fee: **$15.00**
Market Order Sale Fee: **$25.00**
Batch and Market Order Processing Fee: **$0.10 per share**

How much stock does the first $50 buy? :
Initial Investment: **$50.00**
 Minus Initial set up: **$5.00**
 Cash Purchase Fee: **$6.00**
 Cash Purchase Processing Fee (per share): **$0.00**
Total Investment: **$39.00**, Sample Stock Price: **$69.54**
Total Shares Purchased: $39.00/$69.54 = **.560828**

Nike, Inc   37

One Bowerman Drive
Beaverton, Oregon 97005
(503) 671-6300
Company website: **www.nike.com**

Company Description

Nike, Inc. is engaged in design, development and marketing of footwear, apparel, equipment and accessory products. It is a seller of athletic footwear and athletic apparel in the world. It sells its products to retail accounts, through Nike-owned retail, including stores and Internet sales, and through a mix of independent distributors and licensees, in over 170 countries around the world. Nike's athletic footwear products are designed primarily for specific athletic use. It also markets footwear designed for aquatic activities, baseball, cheerleading, football, golf, lacrosse, outdoor activities, skateboarding, tennis, volleyball, walking, wrestling, and other athletic and recreational uses. It also markets apparel with licensed college and professional team, and league logos. It sells a line of performance equipment under the Nike brand name, including bags, socks, sport balls, eyewear, timepieces, electronic devices, bats, gloves and protective equipment.

Basic Company Statistics

New York Stock Exchange: **NKE**

Industry: **Apparel & Footwear**

Index Membership: **S&P 500**

Annual Revenue: **$19 Billion**

Market Capitalization: **$32.3 Billion (Large-Cap)**

Common Shares Outstanding: **477.9 Million**

Earnings per Share: **$3.86**

Annual Dividend: **$1.08**

Paying Dividends Since: **1984**

Direct Stock Purchase Plan Summary

Transfer Agent: **Computershare**
Transfer Agent website: www-us.computershare.com
Phone: 1-800-756-8200

New Account Investment Options:
One-time minimum purchase by either a check or an authorized one-time deduction from a savings or checking account: **$500.00** or the **$500.00** is waived with a minimum on-going investment of **$50.00** for 10 consecutive months.

Existing Shareholders:
Minimum share required to enroll for existing shareholders: **1**
Optional Cash Purchase Minimum: **$50.00**
Optional Cash Purchase Frequency: **Weekly**
Maximum One Time Investment: **$250,000.00 per year**
Stock Certificate issued upon request: **Yes**
Dividend Frequency: **Quarterly**

Plan Fees:
Initial Set up Fee: **$10.00**
Cash Purchase Fee: **$5.00**
On-going Automatic Investment Fee: **$2.00**
Cash Purchase Processing Fee (per share): **$0.03**
Dividend Reinvestment Fee: **5% up to a maximum of $3.00**
Batch Order Sale Fee: **$15.00**
Market Order Sale Fee: **$25.00**
Batch and Market Order Processing Fee: **$0.12 per share**

How much stock does the first $50 buy? :
Initial Investment: **$50.00**
  Minus Initial Set up Fee: **$10.00**
  Cash Purchase Fee: **$5.00**
  Cash Purchase Processing Fee (per share): **$0.03**
Total Investment: **$34.97**, Sample Stock Price: **$83.20**
Total Shares Purchased: $34.97/$83.20 = **.420313**

Phillip Morris International, Inc.   38

120 Park Avenue
New York, New York 10017
(917) 663-2000
Company website: **www.pmi.com**

Company Description

Philip Morris International Inc. is engaged in the manufacture and sale of cigarettes and other tobacco products through its subsidiaries and affiliates. The company's products are sold in approximately 160 countries. PMI's portfolio comprises both international and local brands. Its portfolio comprises both international and local brands, which include Marlboro, Merit, Parliament, Virginia Slims, L&M, Chesterfield, Bond Street, Lark, Muratti, Next, Philip Morris and Red & White. The company divides its markets into four geographic regions: The European Union (EU); The Eastern Europe, Middle East and Africa (EEMA); The Asian Region, and The Latin America and Canada Region. As of December 31, 2009, PMI operated and owned 58 manufacturing facilities, operated two leased manufacturing facilities, one in Korea and one in Mexico, and maintained 30 contract manufacturing relationships with third parties. In September 2009, PMI acquired Swedish Match South Africa (Proprietary) Limited.

Basic Company Statistics

New York Stock Exchange: **PM**

Industry: **Tobacco Products**

Index Membership: **S&P 500**

Annual Revenue: **$25.03 Billion**

Market Capitalization: **$107.2 Billion (Large-Cap)**

Common Shares Outstanding: **1.83 Billion**

Earnings per Share: **$3.24**

Annual Dividend: **$2.56**

Paying Dividends Since: **2008**

Direct Stock Purchase Plan Summary

Transfer Agent: **Computershare**
Transfer Agent website: www-us.computershare.com
Phone: 1-877-745-9350

New Account Investment Options:
One-time minimum purchase by either a check or an authorized one-time deduction from a savings or checking account: **$500.00** or the **$500.00** is waived with a minimum on-going investment of **$50.00** for 10 consecutive months.

Existing Shareholders:
Minimum share required to enroll for existing shareholders: **1**
Optional Cash Purchase Minimum: **$50.00**
Optional Cash Purchase Frequency: **Weekly**
Maximum One Time Investment: **$250,000.00 per year**
Stock Certificate issued upon request: **Yes**
Dividend Frequency: **Quarterly**

Plan Fees:
Initial Set up Fee: **$10.00**
Cash Purchase Fee: **$5.00**
On-going Automatic Investment Fee: **$2.50**
Cash Purchase Processing Fee (per share): **$0.03**
Dividend Reinvestment Fee: 5% **up to a maximum of $3.00**
Batch Sale Fee: **$15.00**
Market Order Sale Fee: **$25.00**
Batch and Market Order Processing Fee: **$0.12 per share**

How much stock does the first $50 buy? :
Initial Investment: **$50.00**
  Minus Initial Set up Fee: **$10.00**
  Cash Purchase Fee: **$5.00**
  Cash Purchase Processing Fee (per share): **$0.03**
Total Investment: **$34.97**, Sample Stock Price: **$59.56**
Total Shares Purchased: $34.97/$59.56 = **.587139**

Staples, Inc.   39

Five Hundred Staples Drive
Framingham, Massachusetts 01702
(508) 253-5000
Company website: **www.staples.com**

Company Description

Staples, Inc. is an office products company. The Company, along with its subsidiaries, offers a range of office products, including supplies, technology, and furniture and business services. It serves customers of all sizes in 25 countries throughout North and South America, Europe, Asia and Australia. The Company operates three business segments: North American Delivery, North American Retail and International Operations.

Basic Company Statistics

NASDAQ: **SPLS**

Industry: **Retail**

Index Memberships: **S&P 500, NASDAQ 100**

Annual Revenue: **$24.2 Billion**

Market Capitalization: **$149.7 Billion (Large-Cap)**

Common Shares Outstanding: **3.98 Billion**

Earnings per Share: **$2.60**

Annual Dividend: **$0.20**

Paying Dividends Since: **1827**

Direct Stock Purchase Plan Summary

Transfer Agent: **Bank of New York Mellon**
Transfer Agent website: www.melloninvestor.com
Phone: 1-800-758-4651

New Account Investment Options:
One-time minimum purchase by either a check or an authorized one-time deduction from a savings or checking account: **$500.00** or the **$500.00** is waived with a minimum on-going investment of **$50.00** for 10 consecutive months.

Existing Shareholders:
Minimum share required to enroll for existing shareholders: **1**
Optional Cash Purchase Minimum: **$50.00**
Optional Cash Purchase Frequency: **Weekly**
Maximum One Time Investment: **$250,000.00 per year**
Stock Certificate issued upon request: **Yes**
Dividend Frequency: **Quarterly**

Plan Fees:
Initial Set up Fee: **$15.00**
Cash Purchase Fee via check: **$5.00**
Cash Purchase Fee via automatic debit: **$2.00**
Cash Purchase Processing Fee (per share): **$0.03**
Dividend Reinvestment Fee: **$0.00**
Market Order Sale Fee: **$15.00**
Market Order Processing Fee: **$0.05 per share**

How much stock does the first $50 buy? :
Initial Investment: **$50.00**
  Minus Initial set up: **$15.00**
  Cash Purchase Fee via automatic debit: **$2.00**
  Cash Purchase Processing Fee (per share): **$0.03**
Total Investment: **$32.97**, Sample Stock Price: **$38.09**
Total Shares Purchased: $32.97/$38.09 = **.7868**

Target Corporation   40

1000 Nicollet Mall
Minneapolis, Minnesota 55403
(612) 304-6073
Company website: **www.targetcorp.com**

Company Description

Target Corporation operates Target general merchandise stores with an assortment of general merchandise and food items. During the fiscal year ended January 30, 2010 (fiscal 2009), the Target stores also included a deeper food assortment, including perishables and an offering of dry, dairy and frozen items. In addition, the Company operates SuperTarget stores with a line of food and general merchandise items. Target.com offers an assortment of general merchandise, including various items found in its stores and a complementary assortment, such as extended sizes and colors, sold only online. It operates in two segments: Retail and Credit Card.

Basic Company Statistics

New York Stock Exchange: **TGT**

Industry: **Retail**

Index Membership: **S&P 500**

Annual Revenue: **$64.9 Billion**

Market Capitalization: **$38.8 Billion (Large-Cap)**

Common Shares Outstanding: **721.4 Million**

Earnings per Share: **$2.86**

Annual Dividend: **$1.00**

Paying Dividends Since: **1965**

Direct Stock Purchase Plan Summary

Transfer Agent: **Bank of New York Mellon**
Transfer Agent website: www.melloninvestor.com
Phone: 1-800-794-9871

New Account Investment Options:
One-time minimum purchase by either a check or an authorized one-time deduction from a savings or checking account: **$500.00** or the **$500.00** is waived with a minimum on-going investment of **$50.00** for 10 consecutive months.

Existing Shareholders:
Minimum share required to enroll for existing shareholders: **1**
Optional Cash Purchase Minimum: **$50.00**
Optional Cash Purchase Frequency: **Weekly**
Maximum One Time Investment: **$250,000.00 per year**
Stock Certificate issued upon request: **Yes**
Dividend Frequency: **Quarterly**

Plan Fees:
Initial Set up Fee: **$10.00**
Cash Purchase Fee via check: **$5.00**
Cash Purchase Fee via automatic debit: **$2.00**
Cash Purchase Processing Fee (per share): **$0.03**
Dividend Reinvestment Fee: **$0.00**
Market Order Sale Fee: **$15.00**
Market Order Processing Fee: **$0.05 per share**

How much stock does the first $50 buy? :
Initial Investment: **$50.00**
  Minus Initial Set up Fee: **$10.00**
  Cash Purchase Fee via automatic debit: **$5.00**
  Cash Purchase Processing Fee: **$0.03**
Total Investment: **$34.97**, Sample Stock Price: **$38.09**
Total Shares Purchased: $34.97/$38.09 = **.9181**

Tiffany & Company   41

727 Fifth Avenue
New York, New York 10022
(212) 755-8000
Company website: **www.tiffany.com**

Company Description

Tiffany & Co. is a holding company and conducts all business through its subsidiary companies. The Company's principal subsidiary, Tiffany and Company, is a jeweler and specialty retailer whose principal merchandise offering is fine jewelry. The Company also sells timepieces, sterling silverware, china, crystal, stationery, fragrances and accessories. Through Tiffany and Company and other subsidiaries, the Company is engaged in product design, manufacturing and retailing activities. Its Americas segment includes sales in Tiffany & Co. stores in the United States, Canada and Latin/South America, as well as sales of Tiffany & Co. products in certain markets through business-to-business, Internet, catalog and wholesale operations. Its Asia-Pacific segment includes sales in Tiffany & Co. stores, as well as sales of Tiffany & Co. products in certain markets through business-to-business, Internet and wholesale operations.

Basic Company Statistics

New York Stock Exchange: **TIF**

Industry: **Retail**

Index Membership: **S&P 500**

Annual Revenue: **$2.86 Billion**

Market Capitalization: **$6.37 Billion (Large-Cap)**

Common Shares Outstanding: **126.3 Million**

Earnings per Share: **$1.74**

Annual Dividend: **$1.00**

Paying Dividends Since: **1988**

Direct Stock Purchase Plan Summary

Transfer Agent: **Bank of New York Mellon**
Transfer Agent website: www.melloninvestor.com
Phone: 1-888-778-1307

New Account Investment Options:
One-time minimum purchase by either a check or an authorized one-time deduction from a savings or checking account: **$250.00** or the **$250.00** is waived with a minimum on-going investment of **$50.00** for 5 consecutive months.

Existing Shareholders:
Minimum share required to enroll for existing shareholders: **1**
Optional Cash Purchase Minimum: **$25.00**
Optional Cash Purchase Frequency: **Weekly**
Maximum One Time Investment: **$100,000.00 per year**
Stock Certificate issued upon request: **Yes**
Dividend Frequency: **Quarterly**

Plan Fees:
Initial Set up Fee: **$15.00**
Cash Purchase Fee via check: **$5.00**
Cash Purchase Fee via automatic debit: **$2.00**
Cash Purchase Processing Fee (per share): **$0.03**
Dividend Reinvestment Fee: **$0.00**
Market Order Sale Fee: **$15.00**
Market Order Processing Fee: **$0.12 per share**

How much stock does the first $50 buy? :
Initial Investment: **$50.00**
  Minus Initial Set up Fee: **$15.00**
  Cash Purchase Fee via automatic debit: **$2.00**
  Cash Purchase Processing Fee (per share): **$0.03**
Total Investment: **$32.97**, Sample Stock Price: **$38.09**
Total Shares Purchased: $32.97/$38.09 = **.7868**

Tyson Foods, Inc. 42

2200 Don Tyson Parkway
Springdale, Arkansas 72762
(479) 290-4000
Company website: **www.tyson.com**

Company Description

Tyson Foods, Inc. is a meat protein and food production company. The Company produces, distributes and markets chicken, beef, pork, prepared foods and related allied products. It operates in four segments: Chicken, Beef, Pork and Prepared Foods. The Company's integrated operations consist of breeding stock, contract growers, feed production, processing, further-processing and marketing and transportation of chicken and related allied products, including animal and pet food ingredients. Through the Company's wholly owned subsidiary, Cobb-Vantress, Inc. (Cobb), it also operates as a poultry breeding stock supplier.

Basic Company Statistics

New York Stock Exchange: **TSN**

Industry: **Meat Products**

Index Membership: **S&P 500**

Annual Revenue: **$26.7 Billion**

Market Capitalization: **$4.8 Billion (Large-Cap)**

Common Shares Outstanding: **377.5 Million**

Earnings per Share: **$2.06**

Annual Dividend: **$0.16**

Paying Dividends Since: **1976**

Direct Stock Purchase Plan Summary

Transfer Agent: **Computershare**
Transfer Agent website: www-us.computershare.com
Phone: 1-877-498-8861

New Account Investment Options:
One-time minimum purchase by either a check or an authorized one-time deduction from a savings or checking account: **$250.00** or the **$250.00** is waived with a minimum on-going investment of **$50.00** for 10 consecutive months.

Existing Shareholders:
Minimum share required to enroll for existing shareholders: **1**
Optional Cash Purchase Minimum: **$50.00**
Optional Cash Purchase Frequency: **Weekly**
Maximum One Time Investment: **$999,999,999.99 per year**
Stock Certificate issued upon request: **Yes**
Dividend Frequency: **Quarterly**

Plan Fees:
Initial Set up Fee: **$7.50**
Cash Purchase Fee: **$5.00**
On-going Automatic Investment Fee: **$2.50**
Cash Purchase Processing Fee (per share): **$0.03**
Dividend Reinvestment Fee: **$0.00**
Batch Order Sale Fee: **$15.00**
Batch Order Processing Fee: **$0.12 per share**

How much stock does the first $50 buy? :
Initial Investment: **$50.00**
  Minus Initial Set up Fee: **$7.50**
  Cash Purchase Fee: **$5.00**
  Cash Purchase Processing Fee (per share): **$0.03**
Total Investment: **$37.47**, Sample Stock Price: **$15.03**
Total Shares Purchased: $37.47/$15.03 = **2.493014**

Union Pacific Corporation 43

1400 Douglas Street
Omaha, Nebraska 68179
(402) 544-5000
Company website: **www.up.com**

Company Description

Union Pacific Corporation is engaged in the transportation business. The Company's operating company, Union Pacific Railroad Company (UPRR), links 23 states in the western two-thirds of the United States. Union Pacific Railroad Company's business mix includes agricultural products, automotive, chemicals, energy, industrial products and intermodal. UPRR has approximately 32,094 route miles, linking Pacific Coast and Gulf Coast ports with the Midwest and eastern United States gateways and providing several corridors to Mexican gateways. The freight traffic consists of bulk, manifest and premium business. Bulk traffic consists of coal, grain, rock, or soda ash in unit trains. Manifest traffic is individual carload or less than train-load business, including commodities, such as lumber, steel, paper and food.

Basic Company Statistics

New York Stock Exchange: **UNP**

Industry: **Railroads**

Index Membership: **S&P 500**

Annual Revenue: **$14.1 Billion**

Market Capitalization: **$44.9 Billion (Large-Cap)**

Common Shares Outstanding: **493.1 Million**

Earnings per Share: **$3.75**

Annual Dividend: **$1.32**

Paying Dividends Since: **1900**

Direct Stock Purchase Plan Summary

Transfer Agent: **Computershare**
Transfer Agent website: www-us.computershare.com
Phone: 1-312-588-4990

New Account Investment Options:
One-time minimum purchase by either a check or an authorized one-time deduction from a savings or checking account: **$250.00** or the **$250.00** is waived with a minimum on-going investment of **$50.00** for 5 consecutive months.

Existing Shareholders:
Minimum share required to enroll for existing shareholders: **1**
Optional Cash Purchase Minimum: **$50.00**
Optional Cash Purchase Frequency: **Weekly**
Maximum One Time Investment: **$250,000.00 per year**
Stock Certificate issued upon request: **Yes**
Dividend Frequency: **Quarterly**

Plan Fees:
Initial Set up Fee: **$0.00**
Cash Purchase Fee: **$0.00**
On-going Automatic Investment Fee: **$0.00**
Cash Purchase Processing Fee (per share): **$0.00**
Dividend Reinvestment Fee: **$0.00**
Batch Order Sale Fee: **$15.00**
Market Order Sale Fee: **$25.00**
Batch and Market Order Processing Fee: **$0.12 per share**

How much stock does the first $50 buy? :
Initial Investment: **$50.00**
  Minus Initial Set up Fee: **$0.00**
  Cash Purchase Fee: **$0.00**
  Cash Purchase Processing Fee (per share): **$0.00**
Total Investment: **$50.00**, Sample Stock Price: **$90.35**
Total Shares Purchased: $50.00/$90.35 = **.553403**

United Technologies Corporation 44

One Financial Plaza
United Technologies Building
Hartford, Connecticut 06101
(860) 728-7000
Company website: **www.utc.com**

Company Description

United Technologies Corporation provides high technology products and services to the building systems and aerospace industries. It operates in six segments: Otis, Carrier, UTC Fire & Security, Pratt & Whitney, Hamilton Sundstrand and Sikorsky. Otis offers elevators, escalators, moving walkways and services. Carrier offers heating, ventilating, air conditioning and refrigeration systems, and equipment, and food service equipment. UTC Fire & Security offers fire and special hazard detection, suppression systems and firefighting equipment, security, monitoring and rapid response systems and service and security personnel services. Pratt & Whitney offers commercial, military, business jet and general aviation aircraft engines, parts and services, industrial gas turbines, geothermal power systems and space propulsion.

Basic Company Statistics

New York Stock Exchange: **UTX**

Industry: **Aerospace & Defense**

Index Memberships: **Dow 30, S&P 500**

Annual Revenue: **$52.9 Billion**

Market Capitalization: **$70.87 Billion (Large-Cap)**

Common Shares Outstanding: **923 Million**

Earnings per Share: **$4.12**

Annual Dividend: **$1.70**

Paying Dividends Since: **1936**

Direct Stock Purchase Plan Summary

Transfer Agent: **Computershare**
Transfer Agent website: www-us.computershare.com
Phone: 1-800-488-9281

New Account Investment Options:
One-time minimum purchase by either a check or an authorized one-time deduction from a savings or checking account: **$250.00** or the **$500.00** is waived with a minimum on-going investment of **$25.00** for 5 consecutive months.

Existing Shareholders:
Minimum share required to enroll for existing shareholders: **1**
Optional Cash Purchase Minimum: **$50.00**
Optional Cash Purchase Frequency: **Weekly**
Maximum One Time Investment: **$120,000.00 per year**
Stock Certificate issued upon request: **Yes**
Dividend Frequency: **Quarterly**

Plan Fees:
Initial Set up Fee: **$10.00**
Cash Purchase Fee: **$5.00**
On-going Automatic Investment Fee: **$2.50**
Cash Purchase Processing Fee (per share): **$0.30**
Dividend Reinvestment Fee: **5% up to a maximum of $3.00**
Batch Order Sale Fee: **$15.00**
Market Order Sale Fee: **$25.00**
Batch and Market Order Processing Fee: **$0.12 per share**

How much stock does the first $50 buy? :
Initial Investment: **$50.00**
  Minus Initial Set up Fee: **$10.00**
  Cash Purchase Fee: **$5.00**
  Cash Purchase Processing Fee (per share): **$0.30**
Total Investment: **$34.70**, Sample Stock Price: **$76.69**
Total Shares Purchased: $34.70/$76.69 = **.452471**

Verizon Communications, Inc.   45

140 West Street
New York, New York 10007
(212) 395-1000
Company website: www.verizon.com

Company Description

Verizon Communications Inc. is a provider of communications services. Verizon operates in two segments: Domestic Wireless and Wireline. Its Domestic Wireless products and services include wireless voice and data services and equipment sales across the United States. Wireline's communications products and services include voice, Internet access, broadband video and data, next generation Internet protocol (IP) network services, network access, long distance and other services. It provides these products and services to consumers in the United States, as well as to carriers, businesses and government customers both in the United States and in 150 other countries worldwide. On January 9, 2009, the company acquired Alltel Corporation (Alltel).

Basic Company Statistics

New York Stock Exchange: **VZ**

Industry: **Telecommunications Services**

Index Memberships: **Dow 30, S&P 500**

Annual Revenue: **$107.8 Billion**

Market Capitalization: **$91.4 Billion (Large-Cap)**

Common Shares Outstanding: **2.82 Billion**

Earnings per Share: **$2.28**

Annual Dividend: **$1.95**

Paying Dividends Since: **1984**

Direct Stock Purchase Plan Summary

Transfer Agent: **Computershare**
Transfer Agent website: www-us.computershare.com
Phone: 1-800-631-2355

New Account Investment Options:
One-time minimum purchase by either a check or an authorized one-time deduction from a savings or checking account: **$250.00** or the **$250.00** is waived with a minimum on-going investment of **$50.00** for 5 consecutive months.

Existing Shareholders:
Minimum share required to enroll for existing shareholders: **1**
Optional Cash Purchase Minimum: **$50.00**
Optional Cash Purchase Frequency: **Weekly**
Maximum One Time Investment: **$200,000.00 per year**
Stock Certificate issued upon request: **Yes**
Dividend Frequency: **Quarterly**

Plan Fees:
Initial Set up Fee: **$0.00**
Cash Purchase Fee: **$0.00**
On-going Automatic Investment Fee: **$0.00**
Cash Purchase Processing Fee (per share): **$0.03**
Dividend Reinvestment Fee: **5% up to a maximum of $2.00**
Batch Order Sale Fee: **$12.50**
Market Order Sale Fee: **$22.50**
Batch and Market Order Processing Fee: **$0.07 per share**

How much stock does the first $50 buy? :
Initial Investment: **$50.00**
  Minus Initial Set up Fee: **$0.00**
  Cash Purchase Fee: **$0.00**
  Cash Purchase Processing Fee (per share): **$0.03**
Total Investment: **$49.97**, Sample Stock Price: **$33.01**
Total Shares Purchased: $49.97/$33.01 = **1.513784**

Wal-Mart Stores, Inc.   46

702 SW Eighth Street
Bentonville, Arkansas 72716
(479) 273-4000
Company website: www.walmartstores.com

Company Description

Wal-Mart Stores, Inc. operates retail stores. The Company operates in three business segments: Wal-mart U.S., International and Sam's Club. During the fiscal year end January 31, 2010, The Wal-mart U.S. segment accounted for 63.8% of its net sales, and operated retail stores in different formats in the United States, as well as Walmart's online retail operations, walmart.com. The International segment consists of retail operations in 14 countries and Puerto Rico. During fiscal 2010, the segment generated 24.7% of the company's net sales. The International segment includes different formats of retail stores and restaurants, including discount stores, super centers and Sam's Clubs that operate outside the United States.

Basic Company Statistics

New York Stock Exchange: **WMT**

Industry: **Retail**

Index Memberships: **Dow 30, S&P 500**

Annual Revenue: **$405.6 Billion**

Market Capitalization: **$196.5 Billion (Large-Cap)**

Common Shares Outstanding: **3.63 Billion**

Earnings per Share: **$3.35**

Annual Dividend: **$1.21**

Paying Dividends Since: **1973**

Direct Stock Purchase Plan Summary

Transfer Agent: **Computershare**
Transfer Agent website: www-us.computershare.com
Phone: 1-800-438-6278

New Account Investment Options:
One-time minimum purchase by either a check or an authorized one-time deduction from a savings or checking account: **$250.00** or the **$250.00** is waived with a minimum on-going investment of **$25.00** for 10 consecutive months.

Existing Shareholders:
Minimum share required to enroll for existing shareholders: **1**
Optional Cash Purchase Minimum: **$50.00**
Optional Cash Purchase Frequency: **Weekly**
Maximum One Time Investment: **$150,000.00 per year**
Stock Certificate issued upon request: **Yes**
Dividend Frequency: **Quarterly**

Plan Fees:
Initial Set up Fee: **$20.00**
Cash Purchase Fee: **$5.00**
On-going Automatic Investment Fee: **$1.00**
Cash Purchase Processing Fee (per share): **$0.05**
Dividend Reinvestment Fee: **$0.00**
Batch Order Sale Fee: **$20.00**
Market Order Sale Fee: **$30.00**
Batch and Market Order Processing Fee: **$0.05 per share**

How much stock does the first $50 buy? :
Initial Investment: **$50.00**
  Minus Initial Set up Fee: **$20.00**
  Cash Purchase Fee: **$5.00**
  Cash Purchase Processing Fee (per share): **$0.05**
Total Investment: **$24.95**, Sample Stock Price: **$55.05**
Total Shares Purchased: $24.95/$55.05 = **.453224**

Waste Management, Inc.   47

1001 Fannin
Suite 4000
Houston, Texas 77002
(713) 512-6200
Company website: **www.wm.com**

Company Description

Waste Management, Inc. is a provider of integrated waste services in North America. Through its subsidiaries, the company provides collection, transfer, recycling, disposal and waste-to-energy services. The company's customers include commercial, industrial, municipal and residential customers, other waste management companies, electric utilities and governmental entities. During the year end December 31, 2009; its largest customer represented approximately 1% of annual revenues. The company manages and evaluates its principal operations through five Groups. The Company's four geographic Groups, which include its Eastern, Midwest, Southern and Western Groups, provide collection, transfer, recycling and disposal services. Its fifth Group is the Wheelabrator Group, which provides waste-to-energy services.

Basic Company Statistics

New York Stock Exchange: **WM**

Industry: **Waste Management**

Index Membership: **S&P 500**

Annual Revenue: **$11.79 Billion**

Market Capitalization: **$16.9 Billion (Large-Cap)**

Common Shares Outstanding: **475.8 Million**

Earnings per Share: **$2.01**

Annual Dividend: **$1.26**

Paying Dividends Since: **1998**

Direct Stock Purchase Plan Summary

Transfer Agent: **Bank of New York Mellon**
Transfer Agent website: www.melloninvestor.com
Phone: 1-800-969-1190

New Account Investment Options:
One-time minimum purchase by either a check or an authorized one-time deduction from a savings or checking account: **$500.00** or the $500.00 is waived with a minimum on-going investment of **$50.00** for 10 consecutive months.

Existing Shareholders:
Minimum share required to enroll for existing shareholders: **1**
Optional Cash Purchase Minimum: **$50.00**
Optional Cash Purchase Frequency: **Weekly**
Maximum One Time Investment: **$100,000.00 per year**
Stock Certificate issued upon request: **Yes**
Dividend Frequency: **Quarterly**

Plan Fees:
Initial Set up Fee: **$10.00**
Cash Purchase Fee via check: **$2.50**
Cash Purchase Fee via automatic debit: **$0.00**
Cash Purchase Processing Fee (per share): **$0.06**
Dividend Reinvestment Fee: **$0.00**
Market Order Sale Fee: **$15.00**
Market Order Processing Fee: **$0.12 per share**

How much stock does the first $50 buy? :
Initial Investment: **$50.00**
 Minus Initial Set up Fee: **$10.00**
  Cash Purchase Fee via automatic debit: **$0.00**
  Cash Purchase Processing Fee (per share): **$0.06**
Total Investment: **$39.94**, Sample Stock Price: **$35.15**
Total Shares Purchased: $39.94/$35.15 = **1.1363**

Weingarten Realty Investors   48

2600 Citadel Plaza Drive
Suite 125
Houston, Texas 77292
(713) 866-6000
Company website: www.weingarten.com

Company Description

Weingarten Realty Investors is a real estate investment trust (REIT) engaged in leasing space to tenants in the shopping and industrial centers. It also manages centers for joint ventures. As of December 31, 2009, the company owned or operated under long-term leases, either directly or through the interest in real estate joint ventures or partnerships, a total of 376 developed income-producing properties and 10 properties under various stages of construction and development. The total number of centers includes 307 neighborhood and community shopping centers located in 22 states spanning the country from coast to coast.

Basic Company Statistics

New York Stock Exchange: **WRI**

Industry: **REIT - Retail**

Index Membership: **S&P 1500**

Annual Revenue: **$577.7 Million**

Market Capitalization: **$3.0 Billion (Mid-Cap)**

Common Shares Outstanding: **120.4 Million**

Earnings per Share: **$1.97**

Annual Dividend: **$1.04**

Paying Dividends Since: **1958**

Direct Stock Purchase Plan Summary

Transfer Agent: **Computershare**
Transfer Agent website: **www-us.computershare.com**
Phone: 1-800-550-4689

New Account Investment Options:
One-time minimum purchase of either a check or an authorized one-time deduction from a savings or checking account: **$250.00** or the **$250.00** is waived with a minimum on-going investment of **$25.00** for 10 consecutive months.

Existing Shareholders:
Minimum share required to enroll for existing shareholders: **1**
Optional Cash Purchase Minimum: **$25.00**
Optional Cash Purchase Frequency: **Weekly**
Maximum One Time Investment: **$300,000.00 per year**
Stock Certificate issued upon request: **Yes**
Dividend Frequency: **Quarterly**

Plan Fees:
Initial Set up Fee: **$10.00**
Cash Purchase Fee: **$5.00**
Check Investment Fee: **$2.00**
Purchase Processing Fee (per share): **$0.06**
Dividend Reinvestment Fee: **$0.00**
Batch Order Sale Fee: **$15.00**
Market Order Sale Fee: **$25.00**
Batch and Market Order Processing: **$0.12 per share**

How much stock does the first $50 buy? :
Initial Investment: **$50.00**
  Minus Initial Set up Fee: **$10.00**
  Cash Purchase Fee: **$5.00**
  Cash Purchase Processing Fee (per share): **$0.06**
Total Investment: **$34.94**. Sample Stock Price: **$24.97**
Total Shares Purchased: $34.94/$24.97 = **1.399279**

Whirlpool Corporation   49

2000 North M-63
Benton Harbor, Michigan 49022
(269) 923-5000
Company website: www.whirlpoolcorp.com

Company Description

Whirlpool Corporation manufactures and markets a range of appliances and related products, primarily for home use. The Company's principal products are laundry appliances, refrigerators, cooking appliances, dishwashers, mixers and other small household appliances. It also produces hermetic compressors for refrigeration systems. Whirlpool manufactures products in 12 countries under 13 principal brand names and markets products worldwide. Whirlpool's geographic segments consist of North America, Europe, Latin America and Asia.

Basic Company Statistics

New York Stock Exchange: **WHR**

Industry: **Appliances**

Index Membership: **S&P 500**

Annual Revenue: **$17 Billion**

Market Capitalization: **$5.8 Billion (Mid-Cap)**

Common Shares Outstanding: **76 Million**

Earnings per Share: **$4.34**

Annual Dividend: **$1.72**

Paying Dividends Since: **1929**

Direct Stock Purchase Plan Summary

Transfer Agent: **Computershare**
Transfer Agent website: www-us.computershare.com
Phone: 1-877-498-8861

New Account Investment Options:
One-time minimum purchase by either a check or an authorized one-time deduction from a savings or checking account: **$250.00** or the **$250.00** is waived with a minimum on-going investment of **$50.00** for 5 consecutive months.

Existing Shareholders:
Minimum share required to enroll for existing shareholders: **1**
Optional Cash Purchase Minimum: **$50.00**
Optional Cash Purchase Frequency: **Weekly**
Maximum One Time Investment: **$250,000.00 per year**
Stock Certificate issued upon request: **Yes**
Dividend Frequency: **Quarterly**

Plan Fees:
Initial Set up Fee: **$5.00**
Cash Purchase Fee: **$5.00**
On-going Automatic Investment Fee: **$2.00**
Cash Purchase Processing Fee (per share): **$0.03**
Dividend Reinvestment Fee: **5% up to a maximum of $3.00**
Batch Order Sale Fee: **$15.00**
Batch Order Processing Fee: **$0.12 per share**

How much stock does the first $50 buy? :
Initial Investment: **$50.00**
  Minus Initial Set up Fee: **$5.00**
  Cash Purchase Fee: **$5.00**
  Cash Purchase Processing Fee (per share): **$.03**
Total Investment: **$39.97**, Sample Stock Price: **$76.45**
Total Shares Purchased: $39.97/$76.45 = **.522825**

Winstream Corporation   50

4001 Rodney Parham Road
Little Rock, Arkansas 72212
(501) 748-7000
Company website: www.windstream.com

Company Description

Windstream Corporation is a telecommunications company that provides phone, high-speed Internet and digital television services. It also offers a range of Internet protocol-based (IP) voice and data services and phone systems and equipment to businesses and government agencies. As of December 31, 2009, it provided service to approximately 3 million access lines and 1.1 million high-speed Internet customers primarily located in rural areas in 16 states. Its wireline segment consists of Windstream's retail and wholesale telecommunications services, whose primary revenue streams include voice and related features, high-speed Internet service, long distance, data and special access, switched access and interconnection and video services.

Basic Company Statistics

New York Stock Exchange: **WIN**

Industry: **Telecommunications Services**

Index Membership: **S&P 500**

Annual Revenue: **$2.99 Billion**

Market Capitalization: **$6.3 Billion (Mid-Cap)**

Common Shares Outstanding: **483.2 Million**

Earnings per Share: **$0.77**

Annual Dividend: **$1.00**

Paying Dividends Since: **2006**

Direct Stock Purchase Plan Summary

Transfer Agent: **Computershare**
Transfer Agent website: www-us.computershare.com
Phone: 1-312-360-5207

New Account Investment Options:
One-time minimum purchase by either a check or an authorized one-time deduction from a savings or checking account: **$250.00** or the **$250.00** is waived with a minimum on-going investment of **$50.00** for 5 consecutive months.

Existing Shareholders:
Minimum share required to enroll for existing shareholders: **1**
Optional Cash Purchase Minimum: **$50.00**
Optional Cash Purchase Frequency: **Weekly**
Maximum One Time Investment: **$250,000.00 per year**
Stock Certificate issued upon request: **Yes**
Dividend Frequency: **Quarterly**

Plan Fees:
Initial Set up Fee: **$10.00**
Cash Purchase Fee: **$5.00**
On-going Automatic Investment Fee: **$2.50**
Cash Purchase Processing Fee (per share): **$0.03**
Dividend Reinvestment Fee: **5% up to a maximum of $3.00**
Batch Order Sale Fee: **$15.00**
Market Order Sale Fee: **$25.00**
Batch and Market Order Processing Fee: **$0.12 per share**

How much stock does the first $50 buy? :
Initial Investment: **$50.00**
  Minus Initial Set up Fee: **$10.00**
  Cash Purchase Fee: **$5.00**
  Cash Purchase Processing Fee (per share): **$.03**
Total Investment: **$34.97**. Sample Stock Price: **$13.02**
Total Shares Purchased: $34.97/$13.02 = **2.685868**

The Stocks by Index

Dow Jones Industrial Average

Company	Industry
Caterpillar, Inc. (CAT)	Construction Machinery
Chevron Corp. (CVX)	Oil & Gas
Coca Cola Company (The) (KO)	Beverages
Exxon Mobil (XOM)	Oil & Gas
Home Depot (The) (HD)	Retail
IBM (IBM)	Information Technology
Intel (INTC)	Information Technology
JPMorgan Chase & Co. (JPM)	Banking
McDonald's Corp (MCD)	Restaurants
United Technologies Corp (UTX)	Aerospace & Defense
Verizon Communications (VZ)	Telecommunications Services
Wal-Mart Stores, Inc. (WMT)	Retail

NASDAQ 100

Company	Industry
Costco Wholesale Corp. (COST)	Retail
Staples, Inc. (SPLS)	Retail

Real Estate Investment Trusts

Company	Industry
Entertainment Prop. Trust (EPR)	REIT-Retail
Colonial Prop. Trust (CLP)	REIT-Residential
Glimcher Realty Trust (GRT)	REIT-Retail
Macerich Company (MAC)	REIT-Retail
Weingarten Realty (WRI)	REIT-Retail

Mid Cap

Company	Industry
Aqua America, Inc. (WTR)	Water Utilities
New York Community (NYB)	Banking

Small Cap

Company	Industry
Bank of South Carolina (BKSC)	Banking
Chemical Financial (CHFC)	Banking

Standard & Poor's 500

Company	Industry
Aetna, Inc. (AET)	Health Care
Altria Group, Inc. (MO)	Tobacco Products
American Electric Power (AEP)	Electric Utilities
Becton Dickinson Co. (BDX)	Health Care Equipment
Best Buy Co., Inc. (BBY)	Retail
Campbell Soup Co. (CPB)	Processed & Packaged Goods
CH Energy Group, Inc. (CHG)	Multi-Utilities
Clorox Co., Inc. (CLX)	Household Products
ConocoPhillips (COP)	Oil & Gas
Dr. Pepper Snapple Group (DPS)	Beverages
Frontier Communications (FTR)	Telecommunications Services
Hershey Company (HSY)	Packaged Foods
JC Penney Co., Inc. (JCP)	Retail
JM Smuckers Co. (SJM)	Processed & Packaged Foods
Kimberly-Clark Corp. (KMB)	Personal Products
Lockheed Martin Corp. (LMT)	Defense Products & Services
Lowe's Companies, Inc. (LOW)	Retail
Newell Rubbermaid (NWL)	House wares & Specialties
Nike, Inc. (NKE)	Apparel & Footwear
Philip Morris (PM)	Tobacco Products
Target Corp. (TGT)	Retail
Tiffany & Co. (TIF)	Retail
Tyson Foods, Inc. (TSN)	Meat Products
Union Pacific Corp. (UNP)	Railroads
Waste Management (WM)	Waste Management
Whirlpool Corp. (WHR)	Appliances
Winstearm Corp. (WIN)	Telecommunications Services

Resources

Here are some websites with information about investing in stocks.

Bloomberg.com – Daily investment and research information. This is a good place for articles on all financial issues.

Cnbc.com – One of the top business news channels and website for research and investment information.

CNN.com/money – Good personal finance site.

Fool.com – An entertaining view of investing in stocks and mutual funds and this is a good place for researching stocks.

Google.com/finance – Daily investment news and research information.

Investing50.com – My blog and website about Direct Stock investing and investment advice.

Investopedia.com – Provides definitions and explains financial terms in plain English.

Kiplinger.com – The best for personal finance information and articles on investment strategies.

Msn.com/moneycentral – Good online tools for portfolio tracking and stock charting.

Thestreet.com – This site grades stocks from A-F and provides investment information and articles.

Tipd.com – A collection of personal finance blogs and investment information written by professional and novice investors.

Yahoo.com/finance – This is a good place to research companies and get the business news of the day.

A Few Good Books

The Wall Street Journal Complete Money and Investing Guidebook, **Dave Kansas**

One Up On Wall Street: How to Use What You Already Know To Make Money in the Market, **Peter Lynch**

Glossary

Annual Report – An annual publication that is produced by a company that provides all the financial information to the shareholders.

Assets – Everything of monetary value that a company or you own.

Batch Order – is an accumulation of all sales requests from shareholders, for a single stock submitted together as a collective request.

Bear Market – A market in which the prices of securities are falling, and the overall market is down. Also, a bear fights by slapping his paws down, thus the phase for a downward market.

Blue Chip Stocks – A large company that has a consistent level of growth in profits and dividends such as IBM, McDonald's and Exxon Mobil.

Book-Entry Securities – Securities that are recorded in electronic records called book entries rather than as paper certificates.

Broker – An individual or firm that charges a fee or commission for executing buy and sell orders of stocks, bonds and mutual funds for investors.

Brokerage Account – An account an investor opens with brokerage firm that allows the investor to deposit funds with the firm and place investment orders through the brokerage, which then carries out the transactions on the investor's behalf.

Bull Market – A market in which the prices of securities are raising, and the overall market is on an upward movement. A bull fights with his horns moving upward, thus the term for stocks moving up ward.

Capital Gain – An increase in the value of an investment such as stock or real estate that gives it a higher worth than the purchase price. The gain is not realized until the asset is sold.

Certificate of Deposit – Also called CDs, is money lent to bank for a set period of time usually three months to five years in exchange in investor will receive a set amount in fixed interest.

Dividend – A share of a company's profits passed on to the shareholders for each share owned, usually paid in cash on a quarterly basis.

Dividend Reinvestment Plan (DRIP) - A plan offered by a publicly traded corporation that allows investors to reinvest their cash dividends, once the investor is the owner of at least one share.

Dividend Yield – A financial ratio that shows how much a company pays out in dividends each year relative to its share price. For example if Company A is trading at $28.00 per share and they pay a dividend of $1.68 per year, then the dividend yield is 6.00%, ($1.68/$28.00=6).

Dollar Cost Averaging – The technique of buying a fixed dollar amount of a particular investment on a regular schedule, regardless of the share price. More shares are purchased when prices are low, and fewer shares are bought when prices are high.

Dow Jones Industrial Average – is a price-weighted average of 30 significant stocks traded on the New York Stock Exchange and the NASDAQ including: Exxon Mobil, Home Depot and Intel.

Earning per Share – The portion of a company's profit allocated to each outstanding share of common stock.

Exchange Traded Fund (ETF) – A security that tracks an index, an industry or a basket of assets like an index fund, but trades like a stock on an exchange.

Holding Company – A parent corporation that owns enough stock in another corporation to control its board of directors and therefore, controls its policies and management.

Index Fund – A type of mutual fund with a portfolio constructed to match or track the components of a market index, such as the S&P 500 Index or the Dow 30.

Individual Retirement Account (IRA) – An investing tool used by individuals to invest money for retirement savings tax free.

Initial Public Offering (IPO) – When a private company sell stock to the public. IPO's are often issued by smaller companies seeking the capital to expand, but they are also done by large privately owned companies looking to become publicly traded.

Market Capitalization – is the total value of a company's outstanding shares times the share price. Market capitalization is calculated by multiplying a company's shares outstanding by the current market price of one share. The stocks of large, medium and small companies are referred to as large-cap, mid-cap, and small-cap, respectively. The current approximate categories of market capitalization are: Large Cap: $10 billion plus, Mid Cap: $2 billion to $10 billion and Small Cap: Less than $2 billion.

Mutual Fund – An investment that is made up of a pool of funds collected from many investors for the purpose of investing in securities such as stocks, bonds and money markets.

Net Profit – A company's total earnings, net profit is calculated by taking revenues and adjusting business expenses, depreciation, interest, taxes and other expenses.

Outstanding Shares – Stock currently held by investors, including restricted shares owned by the company's officers and insiders, as well as those held by the public.

Price Earnings Ratio – A valuation ratio of a company's current share price compared to its per-share earnings. For example, if a company is currently trading at $43 a share and earnings over the last 12 months were $1.95 per share, the P/E ratio for the stock would be 22.05 ($43/$1.95).

Publicly Traded Company – A company that has issued securities through an initial public offering (IPO) and is traded on at least one stock exchange or in the over the counter market.

Registered Shareholder – A list of active owners of a company's shares of stock, updated on an ongoing basis. The register includes each person's name, address and number of shares held.

Return on Investment – A performance measure used to evaluate the efficiency of an investment. To calculate ROI, the income of an investment is divided by the cost of the investment.

Security Exchange Commission (SEC) – A Government commissions created by Congress to regulate the securities markets and protect investors.

Shares – A unit of ownership in a company or mutual fund, which entitles the investor to a share of the profits in the form of a dividend.

Stock Exchange – Securities, commodities, mutual funds and other financial instruments are traded. Exchanges give companies, governments and other groups a platform to sell securities to the investing public.

Street Name – When securities are held in the name of a broker as opposed to holding them in the customer's name.

About the Author

Mkemo London has been investing in stock market and Direct Stock Purchase Plans for over 17 years; he has held several financial positions in a number of companies. He has written many articles on money management, personal finance and investing. He is also a veteran of the United States Navy and resides in New Jersey.